COPING WITH AFRICA'S REFUGEE BURDEN: A TIME FOR SOLUTIONS

COPING WITH AFRICA'S REFUGEE BURDEN: A TIME FOR SOLUTIONS

By
Robert F. Gorman

1987 **MARTINUS NIJHOFF PUBLISHERS**
a member of the KLUWER ACADEMIC PUBLISHERS GROUP
DORDRECHT / BOSTON / LANCASTER
and
UNITAR

Distributors

for the United States and Canada: Kluwer Academic Publishers, P.O. Box 358, Accord Station, Hingham, MA 02018-0358, USA
for the UK and Ireland: Kluwer Academic Publishers, MTP Press Limited, Falcon House, Queen Square, Lancaster LA1 1RN, UK
for all other countries: Kluwer Academic Publishers Group, Distribution Center, P.O. Box 322, 3300 AH Dordrecht, The Netherlands

Library of Congress Cataloging in Publication Data

Gorman, Robert F.
  Coping with Africa's refugee burden.

  Bibliography: p.
  Includes index.
  1. Refugees--Africa. 2. Economic assistance--Africa.
I. Title.
HV640.4.A35G67 1987   362.8'7'096   86-28591
ISBN 90-247-3457-6

ISBN 90-247-3457-6
UN Sales Nr. E.87.XV.RS/15

Book Information

Cover photograph: Ethiopian refugees at Bihin, Somalia. Reproduced from *Refugees* 32 (August 1986), with kind permission of the United Nations High Commissioner for Refugees (UNHCR).

Copyright

PRINTED IN THE NETHERLANDS

To Mary

Foreword

The United Nations Institute for Training and Research (UNITAR) is an autonomous institution within the framework of the United Nations, established to enhance the effectiveness of the United Nations, through appropriate training and research programmes.

The activities of the Institute relate to the functions and objectives of the United Nations and contribute to the maintenance of peace and security as well as to the promotion of economic and social development. Such activities give appropriate priority to the requirements of the Secretary-General and of United Nations organs and specialized agencies.

The economic recovery and development of the African continent has become one of the priority concerns of the international community in recent years. The United Nations system is deeply involved in these efforts. The General Assembly, at its thirteenth special session in 1986, adopted a Programme of Action for African Economic Recovery and Development for the period 1986–1990. The programme includes measures to deal with the plight of the very large numbers of refugees and returnees and the burden imposed by them on the weak economies of many African states.

Because of the very serious nature of the refugee problem in Africa, UNITAR is pleased to publish this study by Professor Robert Gorman of Southwest Texas State University. Professor Gorman provides general background information on the refugee problem in Africa and describes in detail the Second International

Conference on Assistance to Refugees in Africa (ICARA II). Of particular interest is his analysis of the response of the international community to ICARA II and his recommendations for improved action in the future.

The views and conclusions in this study are the responsibility of the author and do not necessarily reflect the opinions of the Board of Trustees or officials of UNITAR. Although UNITAR takes no position on the views and conclusions of the authors of its studies, it does assume responsibility for determing whether a study merits publication.

Michel Doo Kingué
United Nations Under-Secretary-General
and Executive Director of UNITAR

Table of Contents

PART TWO: LINKING REFUGEE AID AND DEVELOPMENT:
THE INTERNATIONAL RESPONSE

Appendices

Preface/Acknowledgements

This book is the product of two years of interaction with individuals on three continents who have labored in the fields of refugee aid and development. It has been a pleasure and an honor for me to have been associated with them in this important work. During this time I have conducted nearly 150 formal interviews and have been in constant informal contact with professionals in the U.N. system, governments, voluntary agencies and the academic world. It is not possible for me to name them all or to describe their various insights and contributions to the research which has led to this book. However, there are several institutions and individuals whose support, assistance and encouragement I cannot fail to acknowledge here. The Council on Foreign Relations made it possible for me to spend a year as an International Affairs Fellow in the U.S. State Department's Refugee Program Bureau where I gained many insights into the evolution of policy on refugee aid and development in the African context. The Ford Foundation subsequently provided support through Africare for me to do the follow-up research on ICARA II which led to the publication of this book. I wish to thank Paul Balaran of the Ford Foundation, whose interest in this subject made this study possible. Special thanks also go to Jim Kelley and Gene Dewey, two remarkable public servants, whose confidence in and support of me helped to get this whole enterprise started, and whose insights have continued to nourish it. I also have benefitted greatly from working with C. Payne Lucas, Joe Kennedy, Kevin Lowther and many other fine people on the staff of Africare. The book has benefitted substantially from comments by Dennis Gallagher and Lance Clark both of whom were kind enough to provide critiques.

Several anonymous reviews provided by a number of U.N. agencies were also very helpful. I would be remiss if I did not thank Michel Doo Kingué and his staff at UNITAR, especially Laurel Isaacs and John Renninger, who made it a pleasure to see this work through to its publication. As always I owe a great debt of thanks to my wife, Mary, and my children, Aaron, Teresa and Ryan for their enduring love and patience, which has made my work so much easier to accomplish. Finally, although this work has benefitted from the thoughts, comments, and suggestions of many people, I alone accept responsibility for any errors or ommissions contained in the following pages.

Robert F. Gorman

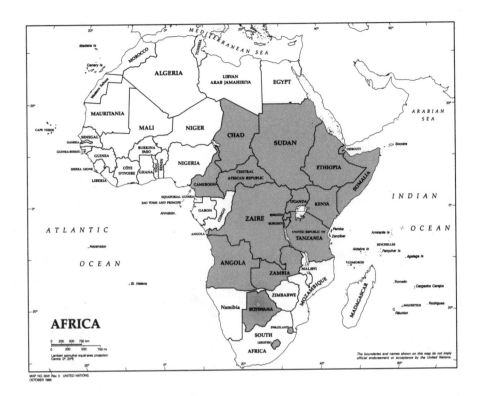

AFRICA

0   250   500   750 km
0   200   500   750 mi
Lambert azimuthal equal-area projection
Centre: 0°, 20°E

The boundaries and names shown on this map do not imply
official endorsement or acceptance by the United Nations.

MAP NO. 3041 Rev. 3   UNITED NATIONS
OCTOBER 1985

ICARA II COUNTRIES

Introduction

There can be little doubt that refugees impose special burden on countries that grant them asylum. Because they are often uprooted suddenly from their homes, rarely do refugees carry with them all of the material possessions necessary to begin a new life in a strange land. Often they arrive penniless, starving and sick. Moreover, when they arrive in large numbers, they often overwhelm the ability of a host government to respond with adequate assistance. Fortunately, the international community usually responds with emergency assistance. But if the immediate physical needs of refugees are met by the generosity of the international community, it is also clear that host governments spend great amounts of time and resources in coping with large influxes of refugees. The economic impact of refugees on the host countries is often obvious but sometimes less tangible. The burdens they generate are numerous, as the following examples from Africa suggest:

- In Gedaref, Sudan, it is estimated that local government officials spend over 60 percent of their time on refugee-related work.
- In Somalia and many other African countries, refugees contribute to the deforestation of wide areas surrounding refugee camps as they search for cooking fuel and building materials.
- Almost everywhere, but especially in Eastern Sudan where refugees compose a sixth or more of the population, already scarce supplies of water for host country nationals are strained even further by the added refugee population.
- Port facilities and roads must accommodate additional wear and tear from use in off-loading and transportation of refugee assistance.

- Local health professionals must accommodate an expanded number of refugee cases. This is especially so where refugees are spontaneously settled outside of refugee camps.
- The need for refugee education, vocational and technical training often places a strain on the teaching manpower and educational resources available to host governments for their own citizens.
- In order to achieve self-sufficiency refugees need suitable land for agricultural activities. But development of agricultural or even range lands to accommodate large numbers of refugees is an expensive proposition for most African countries of asylum.

As these examples suggest, refugees can have a significant impact on the economic and social infrastructure of host countries. This has been a fact of life for many years. But only recently has the international community developed a general awareness of the problem, and tried to address it in a systematic and forthright manner. One of the purposes of this book is to trace the emergence of this awareness. To that end, Part I of this book is devoted to a discussion of the relationship of refugee aid and development assistance, and the efforts of the international community to understand and address it. By far the most important event in the evolution of international thinking on this subject was the Second International Conference on Assistance to Refugees in Africa (ICARA II). Part I examines the evolution of events that led to ICARA II as well as the major goals and themes of this important conference.

Recognizing that ICARA II was but a first step in refugee and development assistance, Part II is devoted to a discussion of the initial response of governments, the U.N. system and non-governmental organizations (NGOs) to the themes addressed by the conference. Several problems are identified which constrain the ability of these actors to respond effectively to ICARA II. It is argued that the two key challenges facing a successful response to ICARA II, will be securing adequate resources on one hand and building effective coordination of development and refugee agencies at all levels.

In Part III, the prospects for the successful linkage of refugee and development assistance are assessed, and recommendations for future action by the international community to ensure a comprehensive response to the refugee burden in Africa are made.

This book is written with the hope that ICARA II was but the beginning of an idea, not merely the climax of a temporary reflex by the international community to African-inspired political pressures. Indeed, one can hope that the global refugee problem will eventually recede, and that the need to address refugee-related development burdens will diminish correspondingly. But for now, and the forseeable future, it is clear that the problems are real and that they require a response. But there are also real difficulties faced by the U.N. system, governments and NGOs as they attempt to respond. Unless the difficulties are squarely identified and dealt with, efforts to link refugee aid and development assistance will fail. As the international community attempts to look beyond ICARA II, then, a hearty sense of realism must temper our hopes for a better future for both refugees and their hosts.

PART ONE

Linking Refugee and Development Assistance
Genesis of the Concept

CHAPTER 1

Refugees and Development

In this chapter, we will review the twin predicaments of the global refugee and development situation, examine the traditional institutional mechanisms established to address them, and review relevant literature that has contributed to the growing awareness of the linkages between refugee and development assistance. It will then be possible in the next chapter to consider the significance of ICARA II more fully.

TWIN PREDICAMENTS:
REFUGEE RELIEF AND DEVELOPMENT

There are about nine to ten million refugees in the world today.[1] Millions more displaced persons find themselves in refugee-like situations but are not classified as refugees because they have not crossed an international border. Most of the world's refugees – indeed about 90 percent of them – and a majority of the displaced persons live in Third World countries. During the period from 1975 to 1981, the global refugee population doubled. Since then it has stabilized. But the traditional preferred solution of voluntary repatriation of refugees has been feasible only in a few cases.[2] Moreover, ongoing political conflict and instability in refugee-producing countries has not only undermined the prospects for voluntary repatriation, but raised the threat of continued refugee flows. In effect, many countries of asylum must face the fact that the refugees are likely to be a long-term burden. Other solutions must be found to resolve the refugees situation and to ease the burden of refugees on host country economies.

If the prospects for voluntary repatriation have not always been bright, some progress nevertheless has been made toward other durable solutions. For instance, about 1.5 million Southeast Asian refugees for whom local settlement was not possible, have been resettled in Western nations. In Africa, where asylum policies are more liberal, the possibilities for third country resettlement are limited but those for local settlement of refugees are better.

Clearly, the search for the most appropriate solution to refugee situations must go on, both for the benefit of refugees and their hosts. Certainly, once emergency relief needs are met, refugee self-reliance should be promoted as early as possible so that they do not become permanent wards of international charity or a continual drain on host country resources. Indeed, a central fact must be recognized as the international community searches for durable solutions to the refugees predicament: excepting the small percentage of refugees who are resettled to other countries, most refugees, either as local settlers or as repatriates, will continue to exert substantial demands on what are almost uniformly weak economies of their receiving countries. In others words, durable solutions can no longer be conceived of as only requiring assistance to the refugees themselves. The impact of large refugee and returnee movements on the economic and social infrastructure of the receiving countries must also be addressed. No longer is it possible to ignore the implications of refugee movements on development. Indeed, the already precarious development status of many Third World countries is only exacerbated by the presence of large numbers of refugees or returnees.

Nowhere is this truth more self-evident than in Africa, where the refugee population has climbed from about 400,000 in the mid-1960s, to 800,000 in the late 1960s, to over 3,000,000 today (and perhaps even more, depending on who one counts as a refugee). Indeed, in the past decade, refugee movements in Africa have grown in both size and intensity. In some cases, literally hundreds of thousands of people have flooded across African boundaries in a matter of a few months, overwhelming the capacity of the host countries to cope with them adequately.[3]

If the global refugee situation seems complex and resistant to quick solutions, the development predicament in much of the Third World is far larger and even more complex. Moreover, in those cases where large numbers of refugees reside in less-developed countries, the predicament takes on the character of a Gordian knot which even the sword of Alexander could scarcely sever with ease. From the massive debt dilemma of middle income countries in Latin America, to the deteriorating economies of many African countries, to the commercial bright spots of Asia, the multi-faceted challenges of development in different Third World contexts seem to confound the experts. Some Third World countries have made tremendous strides in recent years, but after decades of assistance programs, the majority of Third World governments – especially those in Africa – have very little to show for the international attention. A large number of them are even worse off today. Many formerly food self-sufficient countries now import large amounts of food. Population rates have climbed dramatically, often washing out the effects of what little economic growth has occurred. Rural development efforts have suffered as attention has focused on the economic growth of urban areas that have swelled in size from rural immigrants in search of work. Food prices have often been maintained at artificially low levels for the benefit of the urban population, thus reducing incentive for farmers to produce and leading to a need for imports to cover domestic production shortfalls. Moreover, the recent global recession saw commodity prices decline and barriers to Third World exports increase, putting many countries that have devoted more acreage for cash crops for export in a hopeless economic bind. Today, more than one quarter of the globe's population lives in the grip of utter poverty and at the very brink of starvation. Internal political instability and external foreign intervention have aggravated the situation in many poor countries. Nor can one ignore the effects of poor management and bad economic policies of Third World governments, whose public sectors are often top-heavy, ponderous, inefficient, and all too often corrupt. In short, as this litany of ills suggests, development for the majority of the Third World has been an elusive, some would even suggest an illusory, goal.[4]

Added to this already lengthy and formidable list of difficulties is the truly dangerous drought that has dessicated much of the African landscape, parched its fields, killed its livestock and produced famine among its people. The potential consequences of the drought are of course very grave and seem to dwarf the problems posed by refugees to their host countries by comparison. But as the international community responds to the immediate relief needs of drought-stricken Africans, it should not overlook the longer term needs for infrastructural assistance in refugee-impacted areas, many of which have also been affected by the drought.

TRADITIONAL INSTITUTIONAL RESPONSES TO
REFUGEE AND DEVELOPMENT ASSISTANCE

The international community has not ignored the twin problems of refugee aid and development assistance. But it has tended in the past to treat them as largely separate and distinct activities. The U.N. system, for instance, divides refugee and development activities between the U.N. High Commissioner for Refugees (UNHCR), which handles the former, and the U.N. Development Program (UNDP), which coordinates the latter. Clearly this division of labor can be justified. The needs of refugees for protection and assistance are not identical with the development needs of a host country population. The UNHCR has proven to be an indispensible advocate for the interests of refugees. In responding to the assistance and protection needs of refugees, it has adopted flexible policies and procedures to adapt quickly to the often fast-paced changes that occur in refugee situations. Sometimes this has called for engaging in development-related activities on behalf of refugees. But the UNHCR has no mandate to conduct general purpose development in Third World countries as a whole. This has been entrusted to the UNDP, which coordinates the work of its sister U.N. agencies. Development work plainly involves a much lengthier time horizon than that normally associated with refugee situations. Refugee crises call for quick, but often temporary, short-term reactions, while development planning calls for a slower, long-term, and more deliberate approach. Although some U.N. agencies, such as the World Food Programme (WFP) and UNICEF, provide both refugee and development assistance, most U.N. agencies tend to concentrate on one or the other and their management styles tend to vary accordingly.

Similar divisions exist in the administrative operations of donor governments and recipient countries. The United States, vests authority for refugee assistance in one agency (the Bureau for Refugee Programs in the U.S. Department of State) and for development assistance in another (the U.S. Agency for International Development, AID). Other donors like Japan, the United Kingdom (UK) and the Federal Republic of Germany (FRG) make administrative distinctions between multilateral assistance, which have separate components for refugee and development assistance, and bilateral assistance, which is usually almost exclusively devoted to development activities. Some host governments follow this pattern by establishing refugee commissions which are distinct from ministries of planning or other development-related, technical ministries (see chapter 6 for more details). Even nongovernmental organizations (NGOs) tend to specialize in either relief or development work, although some are involved in both activities.

Maintaining this kind of division between development and relief activities may make sense during refugee emergencies or when the refugee situation can be solved expeditiously through voluntary repatriation or third country resettlement. But such an approach has decreasing utility in those cases where voluntary repatriation is not immediately feasible and where local settlement in the country of first asylum is the only available solution. Under such circumstances the long-term burdens that refugees pose for development are more serious and not easily accommodated by administrative arrangements that divide refugee and development functions.

Of course, the distinctions between relief and development agencies of the U.N. system and governments have never been so rigid as to prevent ad hoc cooperation, consultation and sometimes even joint action to meet specific development-related objectives in refugee-impacted areas. But the agendas, operating styles, and bureaucratic instincts of relief and development agencies vary considerably and pose problems for any systematic effort to address refugee-related development issues.

GENESIS OF THE REFUGEE AID AND DEVELOPMENT CONCEPT

The tendency of governments and international agencies to make a distinction between refugee relief and development assistance until recently has been shared by students of the two subjects. However, in recent years the subject of refugees in development has received expanded attention. There is substantial literature on refugee settlements and self-reliance activities.[5] A large number of case studies have focused on specific development problems associated with refugees in particular countries of asylum.[6] Indeed, there has been a growing awareness that a host country's development strategy should begin to take into account the development impact of large rural refugee populations.[7] This literature has dealt at least indirectly with the question of refugee aid and development, although only recently has there been an effort to treat the subject as a distinct field of study.

An important conceptual evolution has occurred in the past two years as the notion of refugee aid and development has been addressed more directly by students of refugees and of development alike. This growing awareness among scholars toward linkages between refugee aid and development was stimulated by parallel developments in the policy-making sphere. Indeed, UNHCR and many governments began to think in the early 1980s about the developmental implications of handling large scale refugee flows.

The implications seemed to fall into two different but hardly unrelated categories. The first set of implications focuses on the refugees and concerns how the international community could provide assistance to them, even during the emergency phase, which should foster rather than foil the emergence of developmentally sound self-reliance programs. Although the assistance given and the policies formulated would focus on the refugees, the host country would benefit from a self-reliant refugee population that could contribute to rather than place a burden on the local economy.

A second set of implications focuses more on the host countries themselves. According to this view, the presence of large numbers of refugees, even where they have achieved self-reliance, imposes a variety of general burdens on a developing country's economy. Although it is clearly legitimate to ask how refugee aid can be channelled in ways that will not be counterproductive to host country development, this perspective frames the question differently: How can development assistance be targeted in ways that will alleviate refugee-related burdens on host country infrastructure?

What these two approaches have in common is their aim to further host country development. But they come at the question from two different directions, one from the standpoint of improving refugee assistance, the other from the standpoint of broadening development assistance so that it addresses refugee-related development needs. Each approach seeks to promote a more integrated understanding of the relationship between relief and development and each calls for greater coordination between refugee and development agencies at all levels to achieve integrated policies and practices. Each perspective has led to a greater appreciation of the linkages between refugee relief and development.

Several international events, emphasizing either one or both of the two perspectives outlined above, helped to shape a growing dialogue involving development officials and other experts on the subject of refugee aid and development. To trace the evolution of this dialogue we must look to Africa itself, for it was there that the refugees posed the most significant challenges to development and there that governments began to recognize and articulate the nature of the refugee burden.

The first stirrings of a development-minded refugee strategy in Africa can be traced to the Conference on the Legal, Economic and Social Aspects of African Refugee Problems, which was held in Addis Ababa in October of 1967 under the auspices of the U.N. Economic Commission for Africa, the Organization for African Unity (OAU), the UNHCR and Sweden's Dag Hammarskjöld Foundation.[8] Among the recommendations of this conference was that African countries hosting refugees, should treat the refugee-affected areas through a zonal development approach. In other words, refugee needs should not be dealt with in isolation from the development needs of the area where they settled. Nor was this seen entirely as a responsibility of the host government. Coordination between the UNHCR, UNDP and other development organizations was also seen as essential. Even before this 1967 conference, zonal development approaches had been experimented with in Burundi and Zaire.[9] However, the concept did not catch hold throughout the continent. Indeed, after the Addis Ababa conference, the zonal development concept languished in relative obscurity for over a decade. In the meantime, however, Africa's refugee problem was growing worse. By 1979 the refugee population more than tripled to over three million from the mere 800,000 that had concerned the delegates at the Addis Ababa conference. Momentum began to build once again for renewed consideration of the African refugee situation.

In May 1979, the Pan African Conference on the Situation of Refugees in Africa, convened in Arusha, Tanzania. Like its predecessor of 1967, this conference was cosponsored by the OAU, the Economic Commission for Africa, and the UNHCR. Despite the precedence of the zonal development concept, ideas about how to promote refugee-related development assistance did not develop fully until after this conference. Nevertheless the Arusha conference did contribute somewhat to the evolution of thinking on refugee-related development aid by introducing the concept of burden sharing.[10] The conference also heightened awareness among the Africans that international assistance was only addressing a fraction of the refugee population in Africa, and largely ignoring the needs of the thousands of spontaneously settled refugees as well as the needs of the host country.[11] The burden sharing concept discussed at Arusha focused initially on promotion of resettlement of some refugees from the most seriously affected asylum countries to other countries in Africa. Later the concept was expanded to include not just resettlement in African countries, but also international assistance to help host countries cope with refugee-related development burdens. The Arusha Conference contributed to this process by underscoring the acute impact refugees, especially spontaneously settled ones, can have in already impoverished areas.

In the year following the Arusha Conference, the government of Sudan convened an International Conference on Refugees in the Sudan, in order to bring to the attention of the international community the tremendous strains that the refugees had placed on its development resources, and to underscore its need for additional assistance.[12] A consensus was building in Africa, that the international community had not given the refugee situation in Africa the attention or the emphasis that it deserved. Momentum began to build for the convening of a conference similar to the July 1979 U.N. Meeting on Refugees and Displaced Persons in Southeast Asia.[13] The upshot was a General Assembly resolution of November 1980 (35/42: See Appendix I) which called for the convening of the International Conference on Assistance to Refugees in Africa (ICARA – an acronym that was later revised to ICARA I after a second conference was called for a few years later) in April of the following year in Geneva, Switzerland.

Held in the wake of an explosion of the African refugee population in the late 1970s, ICARA I had three purposes:
1. to increase international attention to the refugee situation in Africa,
2. to mobilize resources for refugee relief and assistance, and
3. to consider assistance to asylum countries to help them cope with the additional burdens placed by refugees on their economic and social infrastructure.

Of the nearly $900 million of requests placed before ICARA I, about a third ($313 million) consisted of projects addressing the third goal.[14] But the time was not ripe for careful consideration of this kind of assistance. Instead, ICARA I focused on the emergency assistance needs of the refugees, themselves, and did little to address the additional development burden facing the asylum countries. As a result, even though ICARA I garnered $562 million in predominantly emergency assistance for refugees (much of which had already been programmed by donors and thus did not represent additional funds) and heightened global awareness, many Africans considered the conference a failure.[15]

The donors took a different view. Many of them saw ICARA I as a huge success. Indeed, as far as the assistance needs of the refugees were concerned, it was a success. These needs, for the most part, have been met since ICARA I. The problem with ICARA I turned on its failure to make any headway on addressing the refugee-related development needs of host countries. The donor countries, which had responded generously to the emergency and relief assistance requests, balked at the idea that they should underwrite what they considered to be poorly prepared and ill-conceived refugee-related development projects. Given the rather short time for preparation prior to ICARA I (about $4\frac{1}{2}$ months), many of the donors believed that the Africans had simply dusted off a group of marginal shelf projects that had failed to attract previous bilateral support. If the donors were suspicious, the Africans were resentful that their own needs, as distinct from those of the refugees, had been ignored so thoroughly at ICARA I.

If ICARA I ended on a bittersweet note for the Africans, it had nevertheless introduced the concept of refugee-related development assistance. As the refugee crisis that loomed over ICARA I began to fade and as agencies working in the field began to recognize the need for refugee self-reliance and development-oriented programs, the concept eventually took root. In addition to the stabilization of the emergency relief needs of refugees, several other factors contributed to closer attention to ICARA I's call for refugee-related development assistance. First, it had become clearer that most of the world's refugees were unlikely candidates for voluntary repatriation and thus would remain in their countries of asylum for some time. Second, most of the asylum countries were poor and unable to absorb the costs of major settlement programs aimed at integrating the refugees. Finally, the refugees, whether settled in integrated communities or maintained in separate camps, represented a continuing and substantial burden on the ability of host countries to provide necessary social services, education, health care, employment and agricultural assistance without compromising the availability of such scarce resources to their own citizens.

Recognition of these factors by governments and international agencies led to a series of post-ICARA I initiatives that began to grapple with the conceptual and practical implications of addressing refugee-related development assistance.

Shortly after ICARA I, the UNCHR fielded a mission to Pakistan to assess the needs of the Afghan refugees and the local population. It found a need for projects that would generate income for refugees and country nationals, while contributing to the economic development of the refugee-impacted regions. UNHCR asked the World Bank to study the situation further. After a year of study, which began with an identification mission to

Pakistan in April 1982, the World Bank made its final recommendations in December of 1983. These were approved by the UNHCR and in January of 1984 the Bank negotiated agreements with the government of Pakistan and the two affected provinces – Baluchistan and the Northwest Frontier – for a $ 20 million program involving a number of projects which are in the process of being funded by donors.[16]

The World Bank project has been an important practical effort to implement the concept of addressing refugee-related development needs. It has furthered thinking and experimentation with this concept. The genius of the project is its linking of the need to promote self-reliance among refugees by providing them with work and income generation opportunities with the need to compensate for the burden that the presence of refugees has placed on water supplies, forests, and transportation systems of the refugee-impacted regions. Refugees and the host country population earn wages while improving watershed and irrigation management and maintaining roads. Whether the project has succeeded in attaining its objectives is as yet uncertain. Indeed, one might expect less than complete success in this first major effort to link refugee aid and development. In any case, it represents a fresh approach to solving some rather difficult but real problems.[17]

At the same time the World Bank project in Pakistan was evolving, attention to the concept of refugee-related development assistance began to assume a somewhat broader focus. In the fall of 1981, for instance, the Executive Committee of the UNHCR suggested that strategies for addressing refugee-related development assistance should be studied more carefully.[18] Since no U.N. agency had a clear mandate to deal with this kind of assistance – which falls between the traditional responsibilities of refugee and development agencies – it was felt that consideration should be given to identifying appropriate avenues of response. Initially, however, the UNHCR took much of the initiative in exploring this emerging concept, and in presenting its ideas in a variety of international fora, including the Organization for Economic Cooperation and Development (OECD).[19] In addition to its regular and informal Executive Committee meetings where the relationship between refugee aid and development has been discussed over the past several years, the UNHCR sponsored a Meeting of

Experts on Refugee Aid and Development, which was held at Mt. Pèlerin, Switzerland in August of 1983. This three day session brought together two dozen individuals from all over the world to share their thoughts and experiences on this subject. They discussed a background paper commissioned by the UNHCR and drafted a final report. Many of the recommendations were later endorsed, some in a revised form, by the October 1984 Meeting of the UNHCR's Executive Committee.[20]

The experts arrived at several key conclusions. First, emergency assistance from the outset should be sensitive to the development needs of both refugees and the host country population. Refugees should be encouraged to achieve self-reliance in food production and be provided income generation opportunities. But this should not be done for the exclusive benefit of refugees. Host country nationals should also benefit from income generation activities. Moreover, the experts recognized that refugees impose substantial burdens in low income areas where inadequate infrastructure exists to cope with the influx of large numbers of people. Hence, the donor community should be prepared to provide additional assistance to countries of asylum to bolster infrastructural capabilities. The experts also recognized that institutional mechanisms for implementing refugee-related development assistance would need to be devised and seemed to favor an expanded role for UNHCR in this regard.[21]

In short, the experts concluded that neither refugee assistance that ignores development nor development assistance that ignores refugee-related burdens can be truly effective over the long run.

Nor had governments been oblivious to these concerns in the meantime. Several West European governments had begun, in response to the World Bank project in Pakistan, to think about how they could facilitate provision of resources to meet refugee-related development needs. Most notable among these were the UK, FRG, and Switzerland. (See Chapter 5). But discussion in Europe was not limited to these countries alone. Indeed the European Communities (EC) also began to study the whole question of refugee aid and development.[22] Nor was the attention limited to Europe. The United States also developed a program for Africa which addressed the need for refugee-related development assistance. Its African Resettlement Services and Facilities Program was a pioneering effort, initiated in 1982 to promote refugee self-reliance activities and to cope with refugee-related burdens placed on water supply and on forests in semi-arid, refugee-impacted areas.[23]

As preparations for ICARA II intensified (these are reviewed in the next chapter), governments discussed refugee and development issues more often and openly. In the UNHCR informal executive committee meetings of January 1984, the primary topic of discussion was refugee aid and development. Several donors presented statements that indicated careful thought about the relationship of these two kinds of assistance.[24] No longer could the subject be ignored, especially with the onset of ICARA II, which, more than any other single event focused international attention on the subject of refugee aid and development assistance.

NOTES

1. See *World Refugee Survey, 1984.* (New York: U.S. Committee for Refugees, 1984).
2. Robert Gorman, 'Refugee Repatriation in Africa', *The World Today,* 40 (October 1984): 436–443.
3. This was perhaps most apparent recently in Eastern Sudan. A similar refugee crises occurred in Somalia in 1980–83.
4. For a dispassionate assessment of the current development predicament in Africa and suggestions on steps to reverse many current problems see; The World Bank, *Toward Sustained Development in Sub-Saharan Africa: A Joint Program of Action* (Washington, D.C.: The World Bank, 1984).
5. See, for instance, Robert Chambers, 'Rural Refugees in Africa: What the Eye Does Not See', *Disasters,* 3 (1979); 381–392; Terence Finley, 'The Permanent Settlement of African Refugees', *International Migration Review,* 13 (1975): 92–105; Brian Neldner, 'Settlement of Rural Refugees in Africa', *Disasters,* 3 (1979): 393–402; Barry Stein, 'Refugees and Economic Activities in Africa', paper presented at the Khartoum Seminar on Refugees (Khartoum, Sudan, September 1982); and Thayer Scudder and Elizabeth Colson, 'From Welfare to Development: A Conceptual Framework for the Analysis of Dislocated People', in Art Hansen and Anthony Oliver Smith, eds., *Involuntary Migration and Resettlement* (Boulder, CO: Westview Press, 1982).
6. See Hanne Christensen, *Survival Strategies for and by Camp Refugees,* United Nations Research Institute for Social Development, Report No.

82.3. Geneva, Switzerland, 1982; Ahmed Karadawi, 'Constraints on Assistance to Refugees; Some Observations from Sudan', *World Development,* 11 (1983): 537–547; Scott Jacobs and Kathy Paar, 'An Assessment of the Economic Integration of Urban Refugees in Port Sudan, Gedaref and Kassala', (Khartoum, Sudan: Office of Refugee Affairs, U.S. Embassy, 1983), and; Stephen Keller, *Uprooting and Social Change: The Role of Refugees in Development* (Dehli: Manohar Book Service, 1984).

7. See Charles B. Keely, *Global Refugee Policy: The Case for a Development-Oriented Strategy* (Washington, D.C.: The Population Council, 1981); and, Robert Chambers, 'Rural Refugees in Africa: Past Experience, Future Pointers', 6 *Disasters* (1982): 21–30.

8. For analysis of this conference see Richard Greenfield, 'The OAU and Africa's Refugees', in Yassin El-Ayouty, ed. *The OAU after Twenty Years* (New York: Praeger, 1984); and Gaim Kibreab, *Reflections on the African Refugee Problem: A Critical Analysis of Some Basic Assumptions* (Uppsala, Sweden, Swedish Institute for African Studies, 1983).

9. For an excellent treatment of the early history of the zonal development concept see, T.F. Betts (edited by Shelley Pitterman), 'Evolution and Promotion of the Integrated Rural Development Approach to Refugee Policy in Africa', *Africa Today,* 31, 1, 1984: 7–24.

10. For details on the Arusha Conference, see; UNHCR, REF/AR/CONF/ Rpt.I, *Report on the Conference on the Situation of Refugees in Africa.* (Arusha,, Tanzania: 1979); and L.G. Eriksson *et al.,* eds., *An Analyzing Account of the Conference on the African Refugee Problem: Arusha, May 1979* (Uppsala, Sweden: Scandinavian Institute of African Studies, 1981). The recommendations of the Arusha Conference were endorsed by the OAU Council of Ministers in July 1979 and by U.N. General Assmbly resolution 34/61 in November of the same year. For a lucid discussion not only about the role of Arusha in the evolution of the discussion on refugee aid and development but about the ICARA process in general see; Dennis Gallagher and Barry Stein, 'ICARA II: Burden Sharing and Durable Solutions' (Washington, D.C.: Refugee Policy Group, 1984) and D. Lance Clark and Barry Stein, 'Documentary Note: The Relationship Between ICARA II and Refugee Aid and Development' (Washington, D.C.: Refugee Policy Group, 1984). The former has since been published in summary form in the International Catholic Migration Committee's (ICMC), *Migration News,* no. 4 (October-December, 1984): 33–44, while the latter has been published in *Migration Today,* 13,1 (1985): 33–38.

11. See UNHCR, REF/AR/CONF/Rpt I for discussion of problem of spontaneously settled refugees.

12. See Government of Sudan, National Committee for Aid to Refugees, *Report: International Conference on Refugees in Sudan* (June 1980).

13. The U.N. Conference on Refugees and Displaced Persons in Southeast Asia was less successful as a pledging conference than as an effort to highlight the refugee situation in that part of the world. Efforts to establish a Fund for Durable Solutions, which would have linked refugee and development as-

sistance over the long term, failed to attract sufficient donor support despite efforts by the UNHCR to promote the proposal which was initially made by Vice-President Mondale who headed the U.S. delegation to the conference. For details on this abortive effort see; UNHCR A/AC.96/569 *Establishment of a UNHCR Fund for Durable Solutions* Executive Committee, Thirtieth sess., (August 1979); and UNHCR A/AC.96/582, Working Group on the UNHCR Fund for Durable Solutions, Executive Committee, Thirty-first sess. (August 1980).

14. See UNHCR, *ICARA: The Refugee Situation in Africa: Assistance Measures Proposed,* Part II, Annex I, p. 75 for details on ICARA I budgetary requests.

15. Javier Pérez de Cuéllar, 'Secretary-General's Statement to Meeting of Donor Countries Concerning 1984 Conference on Refugees in Africa'. Economic Commission for Africa, Information Service, Press Release No. 2725, (25 February 1983). See also, Omer Birido, 'International Conference on Assistance to Refugees in Africa (ICARA) and its Aftermath', Khartoum Refugee Seminar, (11–14 September 1982).

16. See World Bank statement to ICARA II, Geneva, Switzerland, July 9–11, 1984; and, Poul Hartling, 'Refugee Aid and Development: Genesis and Treating of a Strategy', in *World Refugee Survey, 1984* (New York: U.S. Committee for Refugees, 1984): 16–19.

17. See World Bank, *Staff Appraisal Report: Pakistan: Income Generating Project for Refugee Areas,* Washington, D.C.: 1983.

18. Hartling, p. 17. The Swedish government had raised the issue initially as one which UNHCR should address.

19. See, for instance; 'The Refugee Problem in a Development Context', prepared by the UNHCR for the OECD (Geneva; 1981) and the remarks of Deputy High Commissioner, William R. Smyser, at the Conference on Refugees and Development held in Berlin, 13–17 September 1982. The Berlin Conference was sponsored by the German Foundation for International Development and brought together representatives of Western governments and voluntary agencies. The issue of refugee-related development assistance was also discussed at the March 1983 Meeting between the OAU Seretariat and Voluntary Agencies in Arusha, the Khartoum Seminar on Refugees held in September 1982, the Symposium on the Problems and Consequences of Refugee Migrations in the Developing World held in Manitoba, Canada in August 1983, and the Conference on Assistance to Refugees: Alternative Viewpoints, held in Oxford England in March 1984. Finally, the important study by Sadruddin Aga Khan, *Study on Human Rights and Massive Exoduses,* United Nations Economic and Social Council, (E/CN.4/1503) Commission on Human Rights, (31 December 1981), should also be cited as an important early contribution to thinking on the connection between refugees and development.

20. For the background paper see; Susan Goodwillie, 'Refugees in the Developing World: A Challenge to the International Community', presented to the Meeting of Experts on Refugee Aid and Development, Mont Pèlerin,

Switzerland, 1983; and, the Office of the UNHCR, *Report of the Meeting of Experts on Refugee Aid and Development*. Mont Pèlerin, Switzerland, 29–31 August 1983. See also the Summary Records of the 375th meeting of the Executive Committee of the UNHCR for country attitudes on the subject of refugee aid and development, as well as on the relationship between the UNDP and UNHCR. A/AC.96/SR375, 18 October 1984.

21. *Report, Meeting of Experts,* p. 3. The experts tended to suggest an expanded role for the UNHCR in this area (See pp. 4–5, paragraphs 20–29 and p. 7, paragraph 42). The UNHCR executive committee, however, reaffirmed the key role of the UNDP in development programming while subscribing to the experts suggestion that the UNHCR play a catalytic role in ensuring adequate attention to refugee elements of potential development programming (see A/AC.96/SR375). The experts had suggested that the UNHCR take a lead role in brokering refugee-related development projects noting almost parenthetically that; 'In addition, the role and experience of such development agencies as UNDP should be borne in mind' (*Report of the Meeting of Experts,* at p. 5). The donors clearly have in mind a more central role for the UNDP and a more peripheral, though still important and catalytic, one for UNHCR in this regard.

22. See, for instance, *The Draft Report on Assistance to Refugees in Developing Countries,* compiled by the Committee on Development and Cooperation for the European Parliament, 1983.

23. The U.S. Congress appropriated $45 million for projects under this program from 1982–1984.

24. See for example, A.E. Dewey, 'Refugee Aid and Development', U.S. Statement to the UNHCR Informal Executive Committee Meetings, (January 1984).

CHAPTER 2

The Evolution of ICARA II

The call for ICARA II by the U.N. General Assembly in December of 1982 can be traced in part to the African group's disappointment with ICARA I's failure to address the refugee-related development needs of African countries of asylum. This, combined with the growing realization that many of Africa's refugee situations were unlikely to be resolved expeditiously, led to pressure for a second conference. As expressed in paragraph 5 of UNGA resolution 37/197, the purposes of ICARA II were three-fold:

(5a) to thoroughly review the results of ICARA I,
(5b) to consider provision of additional international assistance to refugees and returnees in Africa for relief, rehabilitation and resettlement, and
(5c) to consider the impact imposed on the national economies of the concerned countries and to provide assistance to strengthen their social and economic infrastructure to cope with the burden of refugees and returnees.

INITIAL REACTIONS

In the view of the African host countries, paragraph 5c was the centerpiece of ICARA II – indeed, the primary justification for the convening of a second conference. But many of the donors remained skeptical about the need for ICARA II, and suspicious of the renewed requests for additional development assistance. Although resolution 37/197 passed by consensus, several donors – some publicly, and others privately – expressed doubts about the need for ICARA II. Unlike the Africans, many donors viewed ICARA I as having been a considerable success, especially in meeting the continuing needs of refugees. As far as refugee assistance was concerned (5b), many donors believed additional resources should be sought through the regular programming exercises of the UNHCR. On this score, many believed that a conference was an unnecessary and expensive proposition. In addition, many donors doubted the potential value of the 5c projects based on the ICARA I experience. The United States in particular emphasized that the 5c projects would have to be well-conceived, based on accurate rather than the inflated refugee estimates used at ICARA I, and focused on a genuine refugee-related need. Moreover, such projects should take into account the absorptive capacity of the host government (that is, its ability to effectively implement such projects) and its ability to meet recurrent costs (that is, costs which projects bring into existence, such as maintenance for roads built, salaries for medical personnel in hospitals constructed, and teaching materials for schools erected). Many donors questioned whether substantial amounts of additional resources could be marshalled to fund such projects, even if they lived up to these criteria.

Most donors indicated they would participate at ICARA II, some without reservations. But many expressed doubts that the exercise would be a useful one. The United States, which is the single largest contributor to refugee programs in Africa, not only expressed skepticism, but withheld announcement of its intention to attend ICARA II for over a year. It was clear that the African enthusiasm for ICARA II was not shared by key donor countries (see chapter 4 for details on the donor position).

LAYING THE GROUNDWORK

It was obvious that conference planners faced a delicate and difficult task in laying the groundwork for a successful conference. Fortunately, they set about their task in a deliberate and well-reasoned fashion. The Secretary-General, pursuant to resolution 37/197, established a Steering Committee, which took responsibility for conference planning. It consisted of representatives from the Secretary-General's office, the Organization of African Unity (OAU), the UNHCR, and the U.N. Development Program (UNDP). High-level officials in each organization were designated to participate in the ongoing work of the Steering Committee. Representing the Secretary-General was Abdulrahim Farah, Under-Secretary-General for Special Political Questions; the U.N. High Commissioner for Refugees by William R. Smyser, Deputy High Commissioner; the Administrator of the UNDP by G. Arthur Brown, Associate Administrator; and, the Chairman of the OAU by Peter Onu, OAU Secretary-General.

The UNDP, although not specifically mentioned in resolution 37/197, was included on the Steering Committee because of the explicitly developmental nature of the 5c projects. One of the major drawbacks of ICARA I had been the lack of UNDP participation. Although some UNDP officials had initial reservations about the wisdom of their participation in ICARA II, as events unfolded it became clear that UNDP participation was essential. Several major donors including the United States insisted that the UNDP must have a role given the predominantly developmental focus of the conference. Indeed, despite early hesitancy, the UNDP began to recognize opportunities in ICARA II to invigorate itself during a period of financial exigency.

With the Steering Committee established and the UNDP on board, planning for ICARA II got underway in the winter and spring of 1983. The first task of the Steering Committee was to develop a set of guidelines which could be used by African asylum countries to develop a conference submission. On March 25, 1983, these guidelines were distributed to UNDP Resident Representatives in Africa. They were shared also with African governments, which were given a deadline of 30 June 1983 to formulate draft submissions for ICARA II.

The guidelines provided a useful outline for governments to follow as they developed submissions in consultation with the UNDP resident representatives and other locally represented U.N. agencies. Governments were asked to address broadly three major areas; 1. government policy in regard to refugees, 2. impact of refugees on the national economy (including such things as infrastructure, food and basic needs, budgetary support, administrative and technical support, use of agricultural and industrial resources, employment, balance-of-payments, and cost of living); and 3. summaries of development projects for consideration at ICARA II (including description of type and number of refugees involved, project costs, project time-frame, assessment of recurrent cost implications, and a justification of each project regarding its relevance to refugees).[1]

From the outset, conference planners recognized the need to stress that development projects presented to ICARA II under the 5c rubric should be directly related to the impact of refugees. In a briefing of donor countries and African asylum nations held in New York on 23 Februay 1983, the Secretary-General stressed that project proposals should be realistic both in terms of their relatedness to refugees and in terms of their cost. Carefully justified proposals would be necessary in order to attract donor support at a time when available resources were limited.

The guidelines reflected the Secretary-General's admonition that careful documentation was needed for both the general refugee burden on the host countries and the particular needs to be addressed by specific projects. If additional resources were to be forthcoming from donors, then the host countries would have to present a convincing, well-documented case. The guidelines were formulated in such a way as to elicit a careful response by host countries. In this way donor skepticism could be overcome, and the mistakes of ICARA I, which included inadequate lead time to develop clearly justified proposals, avoided.

Of the twenty-two African refugee-impacted countries that were invited to submit proposals for infrastructural assistance, fourteen responded by the July deadline. These included; Angola, Botswana, Burundi, Ethiopia, Kenya, Lesotho, Rwanda, Somalia, Sudan, Swaziland, Tanzania, Uganda, Zaire and Zambia. (Six additional countries made requests following ICARA II; Cameroon, Benin, Guinea, Djibouti, Chad, and the Central African Republic. Five of these countries were visited by a U.N. technical team after ICARA II.)

A technical team, consisting of experts drawn from various U.N. agencies, including the UNDP, UNHCR and the Food and Agricultural Organization (FAO), among others, visited each of the fourteen countries that submitted 5c proposals. The technical team was headed by David Feldman, who was seconded by UNDP to the Secretary-General's Office to work with Under-Secretary-General Farah. The technical team met with relevant governmental ministries and departments in each host country. When possible they met with NGO representatives, resident representatives of appropriate U.N. agencies and donor country officials to discuss the host countries' ICARA II submissions.[2]

Although the role of the technical team and the quality of its final country reports have come under criticism from some quarters, its contribution to the success of ICARA II cannot be minimized. The primary task of the technical team was to fulfill the directives of resolution 37/197, which called on the Secretary-General, *et al.*, to submit a report on the impact of the refugee situation in each country, to identify the humanitarian, rehabilitation and resettlement needs of the refugees themselves, and the refugee-related infrastructural assistance needs of the host countries. These needs were also to be identified by priority. The technical team's job in fulfilling this directive was to produce a written report based on the guidelines submitted to host governments documenting the general situation in each country, identifying specific assistance needs by priority, and justifying the refugee-related character of these needs. It followed that the host country should approve fully the final reports.

But if these general principles provided a basic work plan for the technical team missions, they nevertheless left it with a great deal of discretion in dealing with the rather diverse group of nations it would visit. Indeed, some of the countries had large refugee populations, others small ones. Some had hosted refugees for many years, others for only a few years. The overall population of these coutries varied widely, from Swaziland with 600,000 to Ethiopia with 32 million. Per capita Gross National Product (GNP) ranged from a low of $120 in Ethiopia to $1,010 in Botswana. (See Table 2.2 for basic data on each country submitting ICARA II proposals.) How much assistance could each country realistically expect to request at ICARA II? How would this be determined? Answers to these questions called not only for considerable technical expertise, but political savoir-faire as well.

Operating without any specific guidance from his superiors on how to determine relative levels of assistance, Feldman devised an informal formula based on the simple and equitable notion that each country was entitled to about $150 worth of infrastructural assistance for each refugee/returnee under its care. This approach had the advantage of giving the technical team an overall target for each country. If a country's initial request was too high, it would be appropriate to pare it down. Conversely, if the initial requests were too low the job of the technical team would be to identify additional project concepts. Table 2.1 illustrates the effect of the Feldman formula on the actual size of requests placed before ICARA II by the African asylum countries. Although the average ICARA II request per refugee/returnee ranges from a low of $88.00 for Angola to a high of $828.00 for Botswana, most countries fell in a range from $100 to $200. Indeed, the bottom line suggests that the average refugee request for ICARA II was $145, remarkably close to the general target of $150.

The major purpose of the technical team visits were to build on the government submissions which various U.N. specialized agencies, principally UNDP through its resident representatives, had helped to formulate, and to produce a nearly final draft submission which could be incorporated as part of the conference documentation that was to be made available to the donor community and other participants prior to ICARA II. The team would try to ensure that the governments had adhered to the guidelines; that the project concepts incorporated in the submissions were refugee-related; that the level of financial requests was reasonable (i.e., in line with the Feldman formula); that the project concepts were adequately costed; that the problem of recurring costs for ongoing project maintenance were addressed; that a capacity to fund sufficient external technical expertise was built into projects where the host country had inadequate managerial capacity to absorb projects and effectively implement them; and to ensure that the projects, if not integrated with existing development plans, would at least not be contradictory to them.

A clear emphasis of this process was that full-fledged proposals would have to be the subject of further discussions between potential donors and the host governments. Indeed, it was not possible in the one to three weeks that the technical team spent in each country to draw up elaborate project proposals. Instead, the idea was to produce an inventory of project concepts, which on

Table 2.1. ICARA II – Article 5c requests.

Country	Number of refugees/ returnees*	ICARA II 5c request in millions of US$	5c request per refugee in US$
Angola	96,000	8.45	88
Botswana	5,000	4.14	828
Burundi	58,000[a]	10.10	174
Ethiopia	220,000[b]	40.09	182
Kenya	6,000	.84	140
Lesotho	11,500[c]	2.50	217
Rwanda	54,000	8.69	124
Somalia	700,000[d]	79.90	114
Sudan	665,000	92.60	139
Swaziland	7,150	1.42	198
Uganda	120,000	35.85	299
United Republic of Tanzania	160,000	28.14	176
Zaire	304,200	38.80	128
Zambia	93,000	10.74	115
Total	2,500,750	362.26	145

* UNHCR estimates as of mid-1983.
[a] Burundi claims a total of 254,000 refugees, but only 58,000 are in continuing need of international assistance.
[b] This includes 70,000 refugees and 150,000 returnees.
[c] This figure includes 1,330 registered refugees and 10.200 spontaneously settled refugees.
[d] This is the Somali government figure. Other sources suggest that a more accurate mid-1983 figure was nearer 500,000.

their face could be justified on both the basis of need and potential feasibility. Participants on the various technical missions have stressed how tentative much of this process was. Often, the technical experts developed project concepts in a matter of hours, based on the best available information, but without trips to the field itself.[3] That is why they stressed that the result of the missions was an inventory of project concepts rather than concrete project proposals.

Despite the technical team's efforts to put the emphasis on the 'concept' rather than the 'project' in the term 'project concept', many donor community officials and Africans still tended to view the project concepts as something more. Some Africans assumed initially that donors should make concrete commitments to specific projects. On the other hand donors, in reviewing the concepts, often concluded that they were deficient. No one, donors argued, would fund projects like them. But that of course was the point, they were not fully vetted projects, nor was it intended that they be. Slowly, as Feldman explained the work of the technical teams in donor and host country briefings in the months before ICARA II, donors and Africans alike began to appreciate that they had much more talking to do with one another in order to determine the feasibility of the project concepts resulting from the initial technical team/host government consultations.

DOCUMENTING THE BURDEN

One of the problems facing the technical team was how to document the refugee burden on asylum countries. It is useful to examine this question more closely, because the major themes of ICARA II were based on the assumption that refugees impose substantial burdens on their host countries. But, as the technical team discovered, this assumption, though widely held, is almost impossible to verify with hard data. Indeed, hard data are simply not available. It would be nice to know, for instance, what the exact costs are that refugees impose on a host country, or how much of a government's manpower and resources are devoted to meeting refugee needs. In addition, should one assume that refugees impose only burdens? Or should one not try to determine the beneficial inputs refugees make to a local economy? Surely, an analysis of the impact of refugees on host countries should take into account both costs and benefits. (See Chapter 5 for more a more detailed analysis of the burden concept.) But the reality is that the data needed to draw such conclusions are not readily available and would require a massive effort to obtain. Consequently, the technical team was forced to rely on aggregate data and a large body of convicing, if impressionistic, evidence to document the refugee burden. This might not be a completely satisfactory approach for econometricians, but, in the absence of better data, there was little else the host countries and technical team could do.[4]

It is clear that the measurement problems described above were widely recognized and accepted as a given by the donor community. The documentation eventually provided in the ICARA II submissions was considered sufficient by most donors to establish the existence of refugee-related development burdens. Indeed, the basic outlines of the burden are not difficult to see, even if specific data are not available to verify it beyond a shadow of doubt.

What is the evidence? Several general indicators can be cited. First, is the number of refugees or returnees. Referring back to Table 2.1, one can see that the numbers varied from 5,000 in Botswana to 700,000 in places like Somalia and Sudan. Eight of the fifteen countries with the largest refugee populations in the world are found in Africa.[5] Algeria, Angola, Somalia, Sudan, Tanzania, Uganda, Zaire and Zambia have refugee populations at or above 100,000. In other words, in terms of sheer numbers, African countries have a substantial refugee problem.

Second, viewed in per capita terms (see Table 2.2), the African refugee situation is even more dramatic. In Somalia, one in every ten persons is a refugee. In Sudan and Djibouti, one in every thirty persons is a refugee. In specific regions of these countries, refugees may account for more than half of the population. These per capita statistics are striking when placed in a developed country context. Consider, for instance, the Somali case where the refugee/host country population ratio is 1:10. If one in every ten persons in the United States were a refugee, it would have 25 million refugees. Such a comparison may be spurious, but it helps to illustrate the magnitude of the impact that large refugee flows can have on already poor countries.

Third, as Table 2.2 illustrates, most of the African asylum countries are exceedingly poor as measured by per capita GNP statistics. Burundi, Ethiopia, Rwanda, Somalia, Tanzania, Uganda and Zaire have per capita GNPs of under $300 a year. Angola, Djibouti and Sudan have annual per capita GNPs of under $500. They have little, in other words, to share with the refugees.

Fourth, the majority of Africa's asylum countries have experienced a decline in their terms of trade and a decrease over the past

Table 2.2. Selected indicators for African countries submitting projects to ICARA II.

Country	Population mid-1981 (millions)	GNP per capita 1981 (1984 US$)	Terms of trade (1975 = 100)		Growth of per capita GDP		Infant mortality rate (ages 0–1) 1981	Life expectancy at birth 1981	Adult literacy rate 1980	Percentage of population with access to safe drinking water 1975
			1970	1980	1960–70 %	1970–80 %				
Angola	7.8	440	68	113	4.8	−9.2	152	42	–	–
Botswana	0.9	1,010	–	–	5.7	13.5	80	57	35	45
Cameroon	8.4	670	117	144	3.7	5.6	109	47	–	26
Burundi	4.2	230	–	–	4.4	2.8	120	45	25	16
CAR	2.3	300	118	108	1.9	3.0	149	44	39	26
Chad	4.5	120	93	100	0.5	−0.2	150	41	15	–
Djibouti	0.3	–	–	–	–	–	–	–	–	–
Ethiopia	32.0	140	151	142	4.4	2.0	145	46	15	6
Guinea	5.4	290	–	–	3.5	3.3	165	45	20	10
Kenya	17.4	420	119	110	6.0	6.5	85	56	47	17
Lesotho	1.4	540	–	–	5.2	7.9	113	52	52	17
Rwanda	5.3	250	125	145	2.7	4.1	137	46	50	35
Somalia	4.4	280	135	97	1.0	3.4	145	39	60	33
Sudan	19.2	380	83	78	1.3	4.4	122	47	32	46
Swaziland	0.6	760	–	–	8.6	4.6	130	54	65	37
Tanzania	19.1	280	103	102	6.0	4.9	101	52	79	39
Uganda	13.0	220	130	136	5.6	−1.7	96	48	52	35
Zaire	29.8	210	200	91	3.4	0.1	110	50	55	16
Zambia	5.8	600	227	100	5.0	0.7	104	51	44	42

Source: World Bank, *World Development Report, 1983* (Washington, D.C., 1983).

decade in the growth of their per capita gross domestic products. In other words, many of these already poor countries are growing poorer.

Given the rudimentary and limited resources these governments have to provide their own people with health, education, and agricultural development programs, it is reasonable to assume that sudden and large influxes of refugees can overwhelm their capacities to respond. International assistance to refugees helps to ease the burden. But many of Africa's refugees are spontaneously settled and receive no direct international assistance. They impose a direct burden on host country infrastructure. Even in cases where refugees receive substantial international assistance, host countries still provide significant administrative support. In addition, refugees compete for jobs, health care, and education with host country nationals. In arid regions, competition between refugees and host country nationals for water and fuelwood can have severe environmental consequences.

These general considerations suggest strongly that refugees impose substantial burdens on their host countries. The challenge before ICARA II was to attack this generally recognized problem with specific projects in refugee-impacted areas. The task of the technical team in consultation with the African governments was both to document the burden and to identify projects that would address it.

One final point should be made before leaving the subject of documenting the refugee burden. While there is little doubt that refugees impose burdens on host country infrastructure in a way that is often inimical to the interests of the immediate host population, it is not at all clear that in every case the best way to address the host population's needs is to build roads, hospitals, and schools or to improve port facilities. These may be attractive projects for host governments and even necessary, but they also may have only a remotely positive impact on the host country population itself. For instance, primary health care is not dependent on the construction of modern hospitals nor is education impossible without school buildings. The key in these areas is the availability of medicines, school materials and trained personnel. In other cases, refugees place a burden on the local job market, limiting wage earning opportunities for country nationals. While many of the ICARA II projects address the general burden on host country infrastructure, they do not always address these specific needs of the host country population. The ICARA II projects are intended, conceptually at least, to benefit both refugees and the host country population. Some do. But many focus heavily on infrastructure building that, by itself, does not really alleviate the immediate burdens borne by nationals of the host country living in heavily refugee-impacted areas. We will return to a discussion of this important question of how to define the burdens addressed by ICARA II in later chapters. For now it is enough to note that although everyone agrees that refugees impose some burdens on their host countries, there are different conceptions about the nature of the burdens and how best to address them.

SELLING THE PRODUCT

As the technical team neared the end of its field missions in December 1983, the Steering Committee began to turn its attention to publicizing and promoting ICARA II. The conference, itself, which had been scheduled to take place in May 1984 was rescheduled for July because the technical team had been unable to complete its field missions by October as originally anticipated. But once the missions were accomplished, a working group of the Steering Committee, chaired by the UNDP, formulated a final draft of the Conference documentation. This was made available to governments in March 1984. But even before this the Steering Committee was preparing a campaign to promote awareness of and support for ICARA II. A two-pronged approach was devised to accomplish this. First, the Steering Committee held a series of briefings and consultations between donor country representatives and the African group in Geneva. Consultations between donor country representatives in the Western Humanitarian Liaison Group (WHLG) were especially important to the ultimate outcome of ICARA II.[6] The WHLG established a subgroup on ICARA II which met periodically. This allowed donors to share their views on ICARA II, and provided a contact point for consultation with the Steering Committee and the African group.

Another important effort to coordinate donor country response to the African submissions to ICARA II was the creation of a clearinghouse to keep donors abreast of indications of support for specific project concepts. The clearinghouse was coordinated in New York out of the Secretary-General's office and in Geneva by the UNHCR. Finally, to complement the Geneva consultation process, the Steering Committee made numerous trips to donor capitals from February through April. These included trips to London, Paris, Bonn, Brussels, Washington, D.C., Ottawa, Tokyo, Canberra and the Gulf States.

Through this consultation process, the outlines of ICARA II began to take shape. Unlike its predecessor, ICARA II was a truly international conference, in part because of its focus on refugee-related development issues transcended the African context. All U.N. Member States were invited to attend, along with representatives of international organizations (IOs) and NGOs. The conference would take place over three days. Its object would be to establish some key understandings about how the international community could address refugee-related development assistance. It was not billed by the Steering Committee as a pledging conference (a concept that many donors opposed), but neither would countries wishing to make specific pledges be discouraged from doing so. In any case, it was hoped that donor countries would take the opportunity to recognize the dimension of the host country burden, and at least express interest in projects which might receive later funding if found to be feasible and in keeping with donor funding priorities.

Two major categories of assistance would be under consideration; additional relief and rehabilitation assistance for refugees (5b) and direct assistance to asylum countries (5c). A total of 128 5c projects worth an estimated $362 million were included in the Conference documentation. After the conference, $67 million in 5c needs were identified in five additional African countries, bringing the 5c total to $429 million.[7] However, only $10.9 million of 5b assistance was requested, owing in large part to the fact that the UNHCR already handles this kind of assistance as a regular part of its annual programming. The need for large amounts of funding in this category was not great, but some additional needs were identified by the UNHCR. They included projects to promote the viability of refugee settlements that already had been or were soon to be turned over to host countries for administration. These projects were folded into its regular 1984 budget plans. Hence the emphasis of ICARA II would remain on the 5c projects.

The Steering Committee adopted a division of labor for promotion of and preparation for ICARA II. The Secretary-General's office assumed responsibility for production of the Conference documentation and communication with governments, including invitations. It also oversaw the work of the technical team and preparation of the final country submissions. The OAU participated in the work of the technical teams. It also focused several of its ministerial meetings on the question of refugee assistance in Africa, and tried to underscore the need for resolution of key political disputes that have given rise to refugees. In principle it was agreed that African governments should avoid policies that produce refugees in the future and that they resolve other outstanding disputes. The UNDP, for its part, was heavily involved at every stage of the preparation of the country submissions, in providing technical advice to governments, in the technical team reviews, and in chairing the working group that prepared conference documentation. Even though UNDP had extremely limited resources to bring to bear on ICARA II, the decision was taken as early as February 1984 that resident representatives, after consultation with host governments, and approval of UNDP headquarters, could commit small amounts of seed money from Indicative Planning Figure (IPF) resources.[8]

In addition to assuming continued responsibility for assessment of the 5b needs of refugees in Africa, the UNHCR established an ICARA II unit headed by Soren Jessen-Peterson as a focal point for UNHCR preparation for ICARA II. The unit performed the donor clearinghouse function in Geneva. It also worked closely with the Africa Bureau and Public Information Section of UNHCR in identifying assistance needs and publicizing ICARA II themes. Promotional materials were produced and several pre-conference tours for journalists to African asylum countries were planned. The UNHCR also participated in the technical team missions and was a key actor in the Steering Committee promotional efforts in donor countries. The ICARA II unit was also a key player in cultivating the interest of NGOs prior to ICARA II. Although the entire Steering Committee participated in briefings for NGO representatives, the long-standing relationship developed between NGOs headquartered in Geneva enabled UNHCR to play a key role in catalyzing NGO support for ICARA II.

To help clarify the goals of ICARA II, the Steering Committee announced during its missions to donor countries that it would draft a document, which, subject to negotiation and approval by governments, could serve as a conference declaration on basic principles. This document would deal both with the need to consider durable solutions to the refugee situations, and to assist host countries with refugee-related development assistance. The UNHCR took the lead in preparing this draft declaration, which was eventually cleared by all members of the Steering Committee prior to being sent to governments in late May 1984. The draft was subsequently reviewed by governments.

The initial draft of the declaration survived with only minor changes after six weeks of negotiations between the HLWG and the African group in Geneva. The most ticklish issue, and the last to be resolved, was whether refugee-related infrastructural assistance provided by donors was to be subject to the additionality test. The Africans had consistently insisted that these resources must be additional to their regular development programs so that the latter would not be depleted to meet refugee-related burdens. Many of the donors preferred no mention at all of additionality, and opposed strongly any reference that might establish the concept as a right of African governments or a duty of donors. The compromise reached was that such assistance 'should be' additional. The conditional nature of this phrase was acceptable to the donors and Africans. With this compromise, which was effected less than a week before the Conference convened, the Draft Declaration and Program of Action was essentially complete.

THE CONFERENCE: A FIRST STEP

Preparation for ICARA II had been undertaken carefully. Indeed, on the substantive side, the issues surrounding refugee-related development assistance and the debate on refugee aid and development had been aired sufficiently to produce an emerging consensus on appropriate steps to address the burdens. ICARA II would prove to be an important fora in which the international community openly could endorse a set of principles and a program of action to address the burdens. Although the Africans rightly expected that ICARA II also would produce tangible resources for specific projects, its most important function would be to gain a philosophical commitment to the notion of refugee-related development assistance. The conference, as both the Steering Committee and many governments stressed both before and during ICARA II, would be but a first step in addressing the longer range burdens. Hence, it would be preferable to have an agreement on principles without large amounts of immediately available resources rather than to obtain substantial resources but no consensus on principles. In reality ICARA II was a success at least in some ways on both counts.

Representatives of 112 nations, dozens of U.N. agencies and 145 NGOs assembled in the Palais des Nations in Geneva to discuss the issues of refugees and development in Africa.[9] As one government after another took the floor to address these issues, it became clear that a consensus had been reached by them on several key points. First, there was a clear recognition of the need for continued assistance to Africa's refugees, and the need energetically to pursue durable solutions for them. Second, there was almost universal agreement that the refugees place a substantial burden on the economic and social infrastructure of African asylum countries – one which is not addressed by direct assistance to the refugees themselves. Third, there was agreement that the international community should provide additional assistance to meet these burdens, so that regular development needs would not be deprived of existing resources. Fourth, there was general agreement that refugee-related development needs should be addressed as a regular part of development programming at the country level. Relatedly, it was generally recognized that this could be accomplished through existing mechanisms (such as the Consultative Groups convened by the World Bank and the donor country roundtables coordinated by the UNDP) thus obviating the need for any new bureaucratic structures. However, it was agreed that a successful response to the burdens would take years of work, and that in implementing such assistance, coordination between refugee and development agencies at every level in the U.N. system, and in donor and host governments would be essential. Finally, post-ICARA II monitoring was to be conducted by the Secretary-General through the UNHCR in the case of 5b projects and through the UNDP in the case of 5c projects. These basic principles were enunciated in the Final Declaration and Program of Action (See Appendix IV) which was adopted by consensus on the last day of the conference.[10]

If a consensus had been reached on several key principles, neither were the actual assistance requests themselves ignored. About $81 million of pledges were announced at ICARA II. About $18.5 million of this was pledged towards UNHCR activities. However, only $2.2 million of this sum was specifically targeted at the additional 5b needs identified by the UNHCR for ICARA II. The rest ($16.3 million) was pledged to the regular UNHCR 1984 Africa program. About $54 million worth of pledges were made toward 5c projects, although in many cases specific projects and countries were not identified.[11] On the other hand, although many countries did not announce a specific level of financial support, several expressed a commitment or intention to fund 5c projects once feasibility studies had been completed. Thus, ICARA II produced some initial revenues (although what percentage was actually additional in character is yet difficult to determine). Moreover, the prospect that more resources would become available down the line seemed very good. So, while only a fifth of the $362 million in 5c assistance requests received initial support, an air of optimism prevailed as President Leo Tindemans announced the adjournment of ICARA II with the descent of his gavel.

LOOKING BEYOND ICARA II

Indeed, the participants at ICARA II almost uniformly viewed the conference as having been a tremendous success. It had avoided polemical issues and contentious political confrontations and instead had stuck to a discussion of the humanitarian features of the refugee situation in Africa. As Leo Tindemans noted in his closing remarks, the debate had been marked by a 'constructive, positive and humanitarian spirit.'[12]

But there was also a strong feeling among conference participants that ICARA II could not be seen as an end unto itself. Rather, it was but a first step, albeit a positive one, in the right direction. The ultimate success of the conference would depend on the willingness and skill of the international community as a whole to implement the provisions of ICARA II. In other words, it would depend on the availability of additional resources and the determination to coordinate refugee and development assistance in the years ahead, not just in Africa, but elsewhere in the Third World where refugees place burdens on the development of host countries.

In the following chapters, I will examine in greater depth the actual response of key international actors as a follow-up to ICARA II (i.e., IOs, NGOs, donor and host governments). I will also suggest what further steps may be necessary to link effectively refugee aid and development assistance. But before doing so, it should be noted here that several obstacles stand in the way of a successful response to ICARA II. They include; 1. the ability of donors to provide adequate additional assistance; 2. the ability of host countries to absorb this assistance effectively; 3. the ability of refugee and development agencies and ministries to coordinate their activities effectively; and 4. the capacity of the international system to maintain the momentum of the refugee aid and development debate in light of the overwhelming drought relief needs of Africa today. These obstacles, though formidable, are hardly insurmountable. An imaginative and major effort by the international community will be required to overcome them. Whether such a commitment can be sustained is yet to be seen. In the following chapters, the response of the international community to the entire ICARA II enterprise, and to the aforementioned obstacles will be examined in greater detail.

NOTES

1. Letter, with annex containing guidelines, from Under-Secretary General for Special Political Questions, Abdulrahim Farah, to UNDP resident representatives, dated 25 March 1983.
2. For a lucid discussion of the technical team's work, see the statement by David Feldman to the ICARA II Donor's meeting of 21/22 March 1984 in Geneva.
3. This observation is based on interviews with technical team participants.
4. For an interesting discussion of the concept of burden-sharing and attendent questions of measurement, see Gallagher and Stein, pp. 14–19, 26.
5. The Gaza Strip and West Bank Palestinians are not included in this calculation. Numbers of refugees are taken from U.S. Committee for Refugees, *World Refugee Survey, 1984,* p. 39.
6. The WHLG in Geneva consists of the following countries: Austria, Belgium, Canada, Denmark, Finland, France, FRG, Greece, Iceland, Ireland, Italy, Japan, Luxembourg, Netherlands, New Zealand, Norway, Portugal, Spain, Sweden, Switzerland, Turkey, the UK, and the USA. The EC Commission is also represented.
7. See U.N. General Assembly, Report of the Seretary-General on ICARA II, A/39/402/Add.1, 5 November 1984, pp. 6–13 for reports of the technical team visit to these additional countries.
8. See letter from the Associate Administrator to UNDP Resident Representatives, dated 24 February 1984, p. 2.
9. For a list of ICARA II participants see A/39/402, 22 August 1984, pp. 6–7.
10. *Ibid.,* pp. 19–24.
11. See, A/39/402/Add.1, 5 November 1984, pp. 14–28 for a description of donor responses to the Secretary-General's request for an update on ICARA II follow-up activities by governments.
12. See A/39/402, p. 15.

PART TWO

Linking Refugee Aid and Development
The International Response

CHAPTER 3

The Role of International Agencies

The U.N. system has played and will continue to play a key role in follow-up to ICARA II. Specifically, U.N. agencies will serve four main functions; 1. promotion of refugee-related development projects; 2. implementation of some of these projects; 3. coordination of projects implemented by governments and NGOs, and; 4. provision of technical assistance to evaluate project needs, determine project feasibility and assess project success.

Under the framework established pursuant to the ICARA II Declaration and Programme of Action, these promotion, implementation, coordination and evaluation functions will be carried out by a number of agencies. The most important functional distinction is that between 5b and 5c projects. The UNHCR will handle programming for the 5b projects, as it always has. Coordination of the 5c projects will be handled by the UNDP, although a multiplicity of actors will be involved with these projects. Both the UNDP and the Steering Committee as a whole will promote the 5c projects. Depending upon the availability of resources, the UNDP may implement some projects itself, but in any case will coordinate the efforts of other implementors. Other U.N. agencies, such as the World Bank will have a role in coordinating 5c assistance through the Consultative Group process. Still others no doubt will be called on to provide specific technical expertise as projects are designed more fully and implemented.

In other words, the U.N. system has an important role to play in making the ICARA II enterprise work. In the following pages I will examine in greater detail the roles of the two key players, i.e., the UNDP and UNHCR, as well as other agencies which will make important contributions. This will be followed by an assessment of specific institutional steps that should be taken to strengthen U.N. system response and to promote the success of ICARA II and the linkage of refugee aid and development.

THE ROLE OF UNDP

For nearly two decades the UNDP has served as the focal point of U.N. efforts to coordinate development assistance to the Third World. It came into being on 1 January 1966, following a decision by the U.N. General Assembly to merge what were at the time two separate U.N. assistance programs – the Expanded Programme of Technical Assistance and the United Nations Special Fund. The purpose of the merger was to provide for broader, more efficient and better coordinated assistance planning in the U.N. system.[1] While many U.N. agencies provide specific kinds of technical assistance to Third World governments, the UNDP, through its resident representatives, has served as the focal point for coordination of U.N. technical assistance activities. In recent years the coordination role of the UNDP multilateral assistance programs has broadened even further. In many areas the UNDP also has served as the vehicle for collaboration between multilateral and bilateral programs.[2] Through the UNDP-sponsored roundtables, donor countries have participated with the host governments and U.N. agencies in charting development strategies. The central coordinating role of the UNDP in development programming is now well-established in U.N. practice, and is widely recognized by donor and host governments.

Despite general recognition of the UNDP coordination role, in recent years it has had difficulty in meeting expanding development needs in the Third World – especially during a recent period of diminished resource availabilities. Because contributions to the UNDP are made on a voluntary basis, it can not be assured of specific levels of future funding – a liability when trying to undertake long-term development programming, which in the case of the UNDP runs on five year planning cycles. Indeed, while contributions rose from $ 406 million in 1975 to $ 716 million in 1979, they dropped to the $ 675 million level during a three year period from 1980–82. Gradual improvement took place in 1983–84 with contributions edging back up near the $ 700 million mark.[3] It is important to note, however, that at the time ICARA II was conceived, and during the preparatory phase for the conference, UNDP revenues were not keeping pace with expanding needs. The initial reluctance of the UNDP to be drawn deeply into refugee-related development activities can be attributed in part to its concern about not overextending its already limited resources.

Added to this, the UNDP had been only a peripheral actor in refugee-related activities, which are under the purview of the UNHCR. Generally, UNDP personnel have viewed refugee assistance as an ephemeral, short-term activity which falls outside of its competence and mandate. Indeed, respecting direct assistance to refugees, it has always been clear that the UNHCR, not the UNDP has the lead responsibility. Nor had UNDP ever thought it to be otherwise. In those situations where UNHCR has had no field representation, the UNDP has exercised the UNHCR's protection function, by virtue of its lead coordination role for U.N. agencies in the field. Except under these circumstances, however, the UNDP generally has not dealt with refugee-related issues.

Despite its initial reluctance, the UNDP took the responsibility of preparing for ICARA II seriously. As noted in the previous chapter, it was an active player in conference preparations, most importantly so in assisting governments with the preparation of the 5c project concepts. In the wake of ICARA II, the UNDP has taken several further steps to fulfill post conference responsibilities assigned to it under paragraphs 11 and 14 of the Declaration and Program of Action.[4]

From an administrative standpoint the most important step taken by UNDP after the conference was to establish a follow-up unit in its regional bureau for Africa. The unit coordinates the collection and dissemination of information on donor and host country 5c activities, tracks progress on project implementation and assists in mobilizing resources for them.[5] In other words, it serves both a clearinghouse and promotional function for ICARA II 5c projects.

The unit got off to a slow start in part because a full time person was not available to administer it until December 1984. However, in January 1985, its activity quickened. After consultations with the outgoing head of the UNHCR now defunct ICARA II unit, it was decided that the UNDP ICARA II unit would initiate a review all the ICARA II projects once again to determine how they related to ongoing UNDP efforts and to see whether some of them could be folded into existing programs. Initial reviews determined that several ICARA II projects dovetailed nicely with ongoing UNDP projects in a number of countries.

In conjunction with this review the UNDP and UNHCR agreed to request their country representatives to conduct a joint field review of ICARA II submissions. Because the refugee and drought situation has been a fluid one, and because nearly two years had passed since many of the projects were first reviewed by the ICARA II technical team, it was felt that such a review was in order. It has helped to clarify whether some projects were still valid, and to identify new needs. Indeed, it is important to emphasize that the ICARA II unit was open to new refugee/returnee related development projects.

While the new ICARA II unit was an essential administrative step, the linchpin in a successful UNDP response to ICARA II will be the resident representatives. The latest review of projects mentioned above has devolved on them. Moreover, as ICARA II projects are implemented and new needs identified, it will be the resident representatives job to monitor the process. This is completely in keeping with their role in the country roundtable process. This process begins with host country preparation of its plans for development programming. In the process of preparing these plans, the host countries draw heavily on information from the relevant U.N. technical assistance agencies, and the expertise of the UNDP. Once a development strategy has been prepared, the host country meets with donor countries to discuss the plans and seek support for them.

Increasingly these fora have become useful in coordinating bilateral and multilateral assistance efforts. They help to reduce the number of projects working at cross purposes, as well as the amount of duplication. It is for these reasons that many of the donor countries represented at ICARA II felt that the roundtables, together with the Consultative Group process, would be especially appropriate vehicles for 5c projects to be considered and evaluated. Indeed, the principle of the complementarity between refugee-related aid and development assistance was under-scored in the ICARA II Declaration and Programme of Action.[6]

Moreover, it was recognized that this complementarity should extend to the structures established to deal with these kinds of assistance. Because of the strong development implications of the 5c projects, it only makes good sense that they should be reviewed as a regular part of the development programming of host countries. Put in a slightly different perspective, it is important that the asylum countries take into account refugee-related infrastructural needs as they formulate their development strategies. The round-tables provide a useful and convenient avenue for this necessary integration. UNDP officials have indicated their willingness to consider ICARA II projects in this framework, at the initiative of host governments. It is not yet clear, however, that they will actively promote their inclusion with host governments, since the latter still have concerns that to do so would compromise the prospects for additionality.

Apart from coordinating implementation of the ICARA II projects, the UNDP could play an important supplemental role in financing them. Although the bulk of ICARA II projects are likely to be funded through bilateral channels, a significant amount of resources will be also channelled through the UNDP. To encourage this, the UNDP has developed a variety of flexible arrangements for project financing.[7]

To begin with, the UNDP has created a special ICARA II trust fund. Under this arrangement, donor countries who do not have the ability to undertake feasibility studies of projects or to imple-ment them bilaterally, can place resources into the trust fund. If the donor so desires, the resources can be contributed without earmaking them for specific countries or projects. This would give the UNDP maximum flexibility in deciding how to use the funds. On the other hand, donors might prefer to place the funds in trust for specific countries and/or projects. In such cases, the UNDP under a management services contract could conduct the techni-cal review of project feasibility, report the results to the donor, and implement the project in consultation with both the donor and host government.

Closely related to this approach is the cost-sharing arrange-ment, which combines resources from a donor country with small amounts of UNDP resources for financing specific projects.

Every aspect of the project, including its objectives, design plan, timing and scope would be undertaken by the UNDP in full consultation with the donor and host governments.

A final vehicle is that of joint financing. Under this arrangement, two or more donors, together with the United Nations, could coordinate their inputs during the life of a project. The donors would have the freedom to channel their resources separately, through bilateral or multilateral channels, or using NGOs. The UNDP would establish a coordinating mechanism to ensure proper timing and application of the various separate inputs.

These different financing procedures have been used widely by the UNDP in its regular development programming. They are clearly relevant to the refugee-related development projects placed before ICARA II as well. Because of the limited availability of UNDP resources, the frequency with which these mechanisms are used will depend on donor country contributions. Some donors have already channelled resources through the UNDP trust fund arrangements. In addition, the Assistant Administrator of the UNDP, G. Arthur Brown, has authorized the use of small amounts of IPF resources as seed money to conduct initial project feasibility studies for ICARA II projects.[8] These will be kept to a minimum, both because of their limited availability, and because they are not additional funds, and hence would reduce resources for existing development programs.

THE ROLE OF UNHCR

In the aftermath of World War II, the United Nations established the International Refugee Organization (IRO) to protect the interests of millions of post war refugees. It continued to function until 1952. However, in 1951 the UNHCR was established and gradually took over the legal protection function for refugees from the IRO.[9] Although the protection function was the dominant concern of the UNHCR for many years, its mandate also extended to assistance. Over time the latter has grown in size and importance. Moreover, with the vast majority of the refugee population having shifted from Europe to the Third World, the UNHCR mandate to promote durable solutions of necessity has required substantially higher assistance outlays. Indeed, on those occasions where the UNHCR has been the only active U.N. agency, it has served the assistance needs not only of refugees, but of people in refugee-like situations, such as displaced persons and drought victims as well.

In short, the UNHCR primary responsibility for protection of and assistance to refugees has not prevented it from becoming involved in development-like activities. Indeed, its responsibility to explore durable solutions, especially voluntary repatriation and local settlement, has required a sensitivity to development needs. For example, the UNHCR has financed refugee settlements in some 14 African countries.[10] Successful refugee settlements require many of the same development inputs as regular settlements do: water systems, health programs, agricultural inputs, education services, etc. Typically, the UNHCR provides assistance to refugee settlements until they reach or have nearly reached self-sufficiency. At that point, which usually takes an average of four years to achieve, the UNHCR hands the settlement over to the host government. Because the UNHCR is not an operational organization, it relies on NGOs and sometimes on counterpart agencies in the host government to implement these rural refugee settlement projects. The food component of refugee relief is usually coordinated by WFP, and other U.N. agencies, such as UNICEF, often implement water development or health components of UNHCR programs. The development expertise and programming capacities of the UNHCR are in fact quite thin. But because of its mandate to pursue durable solutions for refugees, it has undertaken energetically the overall coordination of refugee settlement activities. Its record in this area has been very good, especially in Africa where local integration is often the only or most feasible option for refugees.

The assistance activities of the UNHCR also extend to rehabilitation for refugees who voluntarily repatriate. This usually takes the form of initial food aid, farm implements, livestock and seed. Again, NGOs usually implement UNHCR returnee programs. In addition, the duration of UNHCR assistance for returnees has in practice rarely exceeded a year. The country of return usually assumes full responsibility after that time for reintegration of returnees.

In short, the UNHCR has a long track record, especially in Africa, of providing development-related resources to further durable solutions for refugees. Short of achieving durable solutions it has tried to promote refugee self-reliance including small-scale argricultural and income generation activities.

Early discussions on the subject of refugee aid and development were marked by mixed sentiments about which U.N. agency should play a lead role in addressing refugee-related development burdens. Many believed that the past performance of the UN-HCR in promoting development-related programs in refugee affected areas qualified it to play the lead role. This was the conclusion made by the UNHCR-sponsored Meeting of Experts on Refugee Aid and Development. But as noted above, neither the donors nor the rest of the U.N. system was prepared to see the UNHCR mandate expanded to include development activities of the sort proposed at ICARA II.

However, if it harbored any hopes for an expanded mandate, the UNHCR yielded in favor of an explicit role for the UNDP respecting the ICARA II 5c projects. As one UNHCR official noted, referring to the UNHCR/UNDP division of responsibility between ICARA II 5b and 5c projects, 'good fences make good neighbors.' Indeed, UNDP/UNHCR collaboration in the planning of ICARA II illustrated each organization's desire to be a good neighbor. Prior to ICARA II, an agreement was reached in a letter of understanding between the two agencies which established guidelines with respect to development activities affecting refugees. (Refer to Appendix VI for a text of this document.) The UNHCR ICARA II unit worked closely with the UNDP after the conference, and facilitated UNDP efforts to establish its own ICARA II follow-up unit.

Within the UNHCR, the emphasis on conference follow-up has shifted from its ICARA II unit back to the Africa Bureau, where ongoing programming for 5b projects will be conducted. But the UNHCR influence on the 5c projects will not cease altogether. In cases where local settlement and voluntary repatriation programs are in train, the UNCHR will be engaged in development-related work. This should be coordinated with infrastructural program activities in refugee-affected areas. Moreover, the UNHCR is often more attuned to the impact of refugees on regional development infrastructure than is the UNDP. As it has demonstrated on numerous occasions, the UNHCR can play a useful 'catalytic' role in identifying such needs and in mobilizing donor support to address them.[11] It should continue to exercise this catalytic function in close communication with UNDP resident representatives in the field. Indeed, at the 34th session of its Executive Committee, the UNHCR submitted a comprehensive document entitled *Refugee Aid and Development,* which reemphasized its continuing role in 5b activities, and its catalytic role in the 5c area.[12] (See Appendix V.)

In this document the UNHCR indicated its willingness to contribute to the cost of existing projects handled by development agencies which might be extended to benefit the refugee population. In such cases its contribution would be in proportion to the percentage of refugees affected. In addition, the UNHCR would be prepared to identify and formulate projects for refugees which would be complementary to existing development projects. As part of this catalytic role, UNHCR would then seek to mobilize resources to finance refugee-related development projects such as these. Implementation would be handled by a relevant development organization and the UNHCR would monitor results for refugees.[13] A similar process would apply in cases where completely new rather than expansions of existing projects are aimed at addressing both the needs of refugees and the host population in the surrounding area. This catalytic role for the UNHCR and the need for coordination with development organizations received the strong support of the Executive Committee.

Indeed, there is evidence that such coordination is possible, as the case of southern Sudan illustrates. There the UNHCR and UNDP established a model working relationship that promoted mutual cooperation in funding and implementation of aerial surveys for a land distribution program, and of water and land development schemes in heavily refugee-impacted areas. Because of political instability in the Southern region, however, the capacity of the U.N. system to follow through on this initially good start at interagency cooperation has been interrupted. Nonetheless, this spirit of cooperation between UNHCR and UNDP needs to be replicated throughout Africa, if the goals of ICARA II are to be achieved.

THE ROLE OF OTHER UNITED NATIONS AGENCIES

Although the UNHCR and UNDP will play the central roles in follow-up to ICARA II, a number of United Nations specialized agencies also will be involved in the process.

The World Bank

Although the World Bank has not focused traditionally on refugees, in recent years it has shown an interest in incorporating refugee related components into its ongoing development efforts. Indeed, the World Bank project in Pakistan has demonstrated how it can become engaged in refugee-related development activities.

In the past the Bank role in refugee affairs has been limited owing to the fact that refugee assistance is provided on a grant rather than a loan basis. This problem can be overcome in a variety of ways. First, if host governments make a direct request to the World Bank, it can fund such projects on a loan basis. Another possibility would be co-financing, in which a donor could bilaterally fund an add-on to a normal World Bank loan program. Finally, the grant versus loan dichotomy does not prevent the Bank from making its expertise available to study the feasibility of refugee-related projects and to determine how well they can be integrated with existing development programs in refugee-affected countries. For instance, the Bank supervised the Tunduru secondary school project in Tanzania from 1977–82. Financing for this project was provided by the UNHCR and the project had the full support of the Tanzanian government. Similarly, at the request of the UNHCR, the Bank undertook design and supervisory functions in the refugee program in Pakistan. In this case the UNHCR was the catalyst in generating international interest in this project, promoting donor contributions to it and monitoring its effects on the refugees. The Bank, on the other hand, works closely with the government of Pakistan in coordinating program implementation.

There is no reason that this model of interagency cooperation with host governments cannot be replicated elsewhere. Indeed, in its statement to ICARA II, the Bank underscored its willingness to provide technical inputs for project development. Clearly the Bank neither desires to nor should it become involved in the direct financing of refugee-related development projects. Indeed, its attention must be focused on the broader needs of developing countries. Nevertheless it is encouraging that the Bank has shown a high-level interest in helping to design development progams that will benefit refugees as well as the host country population.[14]

Finally, the Bank plays an important role in coordinating over-all development planning through the Consultative Group (CG) process. Especially in the heavily refugee-affected countries, the CGs will provide a vehicle for integrating refugee-related de-velopment programming with the overall development strategy of host governments.

The Food and Agricultural Organization (FAO)

The FAO participated fully in the technical team reviews of ICARA II country submissions. About $ 87 million of the original $ 362 million of requests made at ICARA II were for projects in the area of agriculture, forestry, and fisheries. Of the $ 67 million in additional requests since ICARA II, about $ 18.5 million are for projects in agriculture. In short, about one quarter of the ICARA II package is devoted to projects which are of direct relevance to the FAO. Indeed, donors interested in refugee-related agricul-tural development projects, fisheries or reforestation might con-sider the FAO as a potential supervisory agency for project im-plementation. FAO has already conducted feasibility and design studies on twenty-three ICARA II projects that fall under its area of expertise and interest. As projects are reviewed and designed FAO will continue to provide useful advisory inputs.

The World Food Programme (WFP)

In its address to ICARA II, the WFP indicated its willingness to provide food assistance where this would be appropriate as a supplement to 5c projects. After reviewing the ICARA II submis-sions, WFP identified several reforestation and road projects in which food-for-work components could be incorporated. They also identified several projects that would be consistent with ongoing programs to which the WFP contributes. Many of these programs are meant to facilitate settlement of refugees and returnees. Indeed, the WFP has contributed $31 million to such programs in Africa. Moreover, WFP's overall expenditures in support of sub-Saharan African development activites at large exceeded $1 billion in 1983. In short, the WFP is in a position both as a result of its work with refugees and development in Africa, to contribute meaningfully to infrastructural projects. In fact, the WFP governing body, the Committee on Food Aid Policies and Programmes (CFA) has supported endeavors to ensure that food aid is applied in ways conducive to strengthening rural infrastructure.[15]

The World Health Organization (WHO)

The impact of refugees on the health care systems and delivery capacities of host governments, can be staggering especially during relief emergencies. But even after emergencies refugees place a strain on the health care infrastructure of host countries. The role of WHO in providing technical assistance to both refugees and the host population is important. Indeed, WHO personnel participated in several of the technical team missions prior to ICARA II.

About 16 percent of the dollar value of projects set before ICARA II were for health related activities. The lion's share of these were for construction of hospitals, despensaries and rural health centers, but some also focused on health training, education, and sanitation. WHO technical support and advice will be important to the successful elaboration of such projects. Indeed, with some funding from UNDP, WHO has already undertaken a feasibility study of an ICARA II health program in Djibouti.

The United Nations Educational, Scientific and Cultural Organization (UNESCO)

Another major component of the ICARA II submissions was in the education sector. Refugees typically place a substantial burden on the educational resources of developing countries. Not surprisingly, about a fifth of the ICARA II package was devoted to education and training programs. UNESCO is heavily involved in such areas as schools, curriculum development, teacher training and language training. Its programs in Africa have addressed the educational needs of both refugees and host country nationals in the past. UNESCO has provided assistance to UNHCR in designing refugee education in Africa. In short, its expertise in this area will be important in assessing project feasibility, and in designing future programs that will address the education, training and cultural needs of the entire population in refugee-affected areas.

The United Nation's Children Fund (UNICEF)

The activities of UNICEF in support of refugees and local people in Africa cuts across sectoral lines. It has been involved in projects promoting health care, sanitation, water supply, education and community development. In countries where other specialized agencies normally in charge of such activity are not represented, UNICEF could provide technical advice for program development or support for project implementation.

Other Agencies

The organizations mentioned above do not constitute an exhaustive list. Many other U.N. agencies could contribute meaningfully to the identification, design, and implementation of ICARA II projects. The International Labour Organisation (ILO), for instance, is involved in income generation programs for refugees in Africa. The United Nations Environment Programme (UNEP) could play a useful role in reforestation programs aimed at addressing the impact of refugees on the host country environment. Similarly, to the extent that infrastructural programs will be coupled with refugee settlement programs, the U.N. Centre for Human Settlements (UNCHS) could have a useful role to play. In Somalia, for example, UNCHS has undertaken a pilot project in low cost housing with funding from the UNDP. Clearly, other organizations in the U.N. system could undertake activities in their special fields of competence at the request of donor or host governments seeking specific technical advice or assistance.

INSTITUTIONAL NEEDS

In general the U.N. system response to ICARA II is on track at this juncture. The institutional machinery to follow-up on linkage of refugee and development assistance is in place, although not necessarily operating at full capacity. The UNDP and UNHCR have mapped out their respective responsibilities for monitoring conference follow-through and agreement exists in principle that existing development planning mechanisms in the host countries could be harnessed to ensure complementarity of refugee and development assistance activities.

The key institutional needs do not require the creation of new bureaucratic structures, but rather the effective coordination of existing mechanisms. The challenge that remains before the U.N. system is to fine tune the ICARA II follow-up process and, ideally, to broaden it beyond the African context.

The key problems that must still be addressed include; overall coordination at the headquarters and field level, ensuring a high quality of U.N. agency field representation, maintaining the visibility of ICARA II themes in the development planning process, and establishing effective U.N. system liaison with NGOs (especially in the case of the UNDP). If these problems are not addressed as a matter of long-term priority, they could stymie a successful U.N. response to ICARA II, notwithstanding the basically sound steps that have been taken thus far. Each of these problems is dealt with in greater detail below.

Coordination

Perhaps the most important aspect of U.N. involvement in ICARA II follow-up will be its coordination of the process. Coordination will be necessary at every level of the U.N. system itself; in the field, at agency headquarters, and between headquarters and the field. Moreover, given the range of governments, international agencies and NGOs that will be involved, overall U.N. coordination of the process will be essential.

As noted before, UNDP will have the honors in coordinating 5c programs. But the UNHCR will continue to play an important advocacy role. Indeed, the UNHCR has shown itself to be more aware of and attentive to the needs of refugees and the local population in refugee affected areas than the UNDP. But its development programming skills have been lacking. The UNDP, on the other hand, while not being as attentive as UNHCR to refugee impacts on host countries, hàs the requisite development expertise and the mandate to address them. In short there is a basic dichotomy between interest or inclination, and expertise or capability to respond to refugee-related development burdens. As we will see in the following chapters, this basic dichotomy is reflected in donor and host country agencies responsible for either refugee or development assistance and planning. Typically, national refugee agencies are more attuned to the refugee impact than development agencies, but lack the ability of the latter to respond comprehensively to them.

Obviously this inclination/capability problem can be answered only if the relevant refugee and development agencies coordinate their activities and communicate on how best to address the refugee-related development burdens that fall between their traditional spheres of activity. In this respect, the UNDP and UNHCR have a major responsibility to collaborate closely on ICARA II follow-up, especially in the field.

Coordination between the UNHCR, UNDP and other relevant U.N. agencies can be accomplished through existing channels. At the headquarters level, ICARA II follow-up will continue to be overseen by the Steering Committee. In the field, UNDP resident representatives will have the lead role in coordinating ICARA II activities. Finally, preparation for the CGs and roundtables between host and donor countries will provide an opportunity for U.N. field representatives in coordination with their headquarters to address ICARA II themes.

Another important aspect of coordination concerns the donor country response to ICARA II. Donors collaborated frequently concerning preparations for the conference. As already noted, a clearinghouse was established to keep donors informed of each other's interests in projects prior to ICARA II. The primary forum for this coordination was the WHLG in Geneva. Now that the focus for the infrastructural projects has shifted to the UNDP and New York, the WHLG mechanism is no longer as conveniently available. And since ICARA II, active donor coordination has slowed to a crawl. The UNDP ICARA II unit now bears much of the brunt for donor coordination, and does seek to stay in touch with country missions to the United Nations. But this has been at best a piecemeal process. What is needed is the establishment of a mechanism in New York similar to that performed by the WHLG in Geneva. This would enhance UNDP capacity to collect and disseminate rapidly information on ICARA II follow-up. As an interim measure the UNDP, perhaps in cooperation with the UNCHR, could use the Geneva-based WHLG as a focal point for donor coordination. Whatever steps are taken, there is a clear need to reestablish direct donor dialogue on ICARA II, so that it remains both a visible item on donor agendas and so that donors can be informed quickly of the status of their respective follow-up activities.

Quality of Field Representation

There can be little doubt that the most crucial need for quality of coordination will be in the field. Ultimately, it is there where ICARA II will succeed or fail. For this reason, it is essential that U.N. representation in African field offices be of the utmost quality. Indeed, the broader problems posed by the drought also call for strengthened U.N. field representation. In recent months the UNDP has taken steps to upgrade its field representation in nine countries affected most seriously by the drought, many which made requests at ICARA II. As more senior UNDP personnel are rotated into these key field positions, one would hope that the refugee-related component of the broader African crisis will remain a matter of priority consideration for them. This raises a third problem: the visibility factor.

The Visibility Factor

ICARA II has had a visibility problem from the very start. Because of the development-oriented themes and longer-term focus of the conference, it had difficulty capturing the same degree of attention from the public media as compared to the recent donor conference on emergency assistance to Africa, which was held in March 1985 in Geneva. Development does not have the same dramatic appeal as starving refugees. The lack of media attention was more pronounced in the United States than in Europe or Africa where development issues have a broader constituency.[16] But if the convening of ICARA II generated only modest publicity initially, it has done little better since.

Perhaps it was inevitable under any circumstances that the visibility of ICARA II would have diminished over time, if for no other reason that that the long-term nature of the enterprise would have been overtaken by bureaucratic routine. But the immediate problem of drought and famine in Africa has drawn international attention away from much needed development efforts of a longer term nature. The energies of U.N. agencies also have been monopolized to a great extent by the drought. The Administrator of the UNDP, Bradford Morse, for instance, was named by U.N. Secretary General Pérez de Cuéllar to coordinate U.N. drought response to Africa.[17] Working closely with him is Under-Secretary General for Special Political Affairs, Abdulrahim Farah. Mr. Farah's office and the UNDP are, of course, key players on ICARA II follow-up as well. Clearly, however, the immediacy of the African famine has limited their ability to focus on ICARA II as forthrightly as they otherwise might.

The visibility problem is hardly limited to the concerned U.N. agencies. Governments, too, have found their resources and attention monopolized by the current emergency. Neither is it clear that the representatives of donor governments or even relevant ministries in African governments are sufficiently aware of what ICARA II stands for. Hence, the need for education on the importance of addressing refugee-related development burdens, which have been only exacerbated by drought, is not limited to the general public alone. ICARA II has a visibility problem with many of the very entities and agencies which are responsible for handling its implementation.

Several steps could be taken by the relevant U.N. actors to ensure that ICARA II does not disappear from the international community's radar screen. First, recognizing that the key to eventual success lies in Africa, the ICARA II Steering Committee should visit key asylum countries to emphasize the importance of the refugee/returnee element in development planning. It should meet with relevant U.N. agencies and if possible with donor and host country representatives to underscore this theme.

Second, a major result of the Steering Committee visits should be the establishment of informal ICARA II Steering groups which would monitor progress on implementation in each host country. These groups would be coordinated by the UNDP and, depending upon the circumstance of each situation, could include participation by representatives of the UNHCR, other relevant U.N. agencies, donor and host countries, and NGOs. The purpose of these informal meetings would be to heighten awareness of relevant actors in each country to the infrastructural assistance needs in refugee-impacted areas. It also could act as a forum in which new projects could be identified and existing projects monitored or reassessed. In many countries, there is already a high degree of collaboration between development and refugee organizations. In these cases, it would be relatively easy to build in an ICARA II component. In any case, the quality of leadership exercised by UNDP resident representatives would be crucial to the success of the ICARA II steering groups.

Third, the Governing Council of the UNDP and Executive Committee of the UNHCR should annually review progress on ICARA II follow-up. Moreover, the Steering Committee should appear at these meetings to emphasize the importance of continued interagency coordination. Similarly, the U.N. General Assembly, should continue its annual review of ICARA II follow-up for as long as necessary.

Fourth, while the current drought has dampened the momentum of ICARA II, it too could be turned to advantage. Certainly it should be clear to the casual observer that the lack of infrastructural development in Africa has been a major contributing factor to the severity of the drought. Moreover, many of the hardest hit areas are also the most seriously refugee-impacted areas as well. The international community must not lose sight of these realities as it responds to the current humanitarian needs of Africa. Indeed, an opportunity exists to use the current wave of concern over the humanitarian emergency as a vehicle for obtaining a longer term commitment to deal with some of the underlying causes of the current dilemma, which includes the widespread lack of adequate infrastructure.

United Nations/NGO Liaison

A final area in which the U.N. system needs to make progress is in dealing effectively with NGOs. This is not to suggest that NGOs and the U.N. system have no relationship. Indeed, many NGOs have been granted consultative status with the United Nations for years.[18] In this capacity, they have provided advice to U.N. agencies and performed a quasi-lobbying function. In addition, several U.N. agencies fund the activities of the Non-Governmental Liaison Service (NGLS), which was created by the Joint United Nations Information Committee (JUNIC).[19] JUNIC, itself, previously coordinated the work of various U.N. agencies involved in some capacity with NGOs.[20] The primary focus of NGLS is in the area of development education and the promotion of a positive public image of the United Nations.[21]

However, if the U.N. system has shown a great deal of superficial rhetorical support for NGOs, this has not always translated into organic working relationships. Indeed, in the development assistance field, operational relations have failed in the main to materialize between U.N. agencies and NGOs. An exception to this is the UNHCR, which has a good track record in using NGOs as implementors of refugee assistance programs. But the rest of the U.N. system has tended to look inward for implementing partners. The UNDP, in particular, has been required to work with its sister agencies in the U.N. system, and has found it difficult to work with NGOs. So it goes with the World Bank and other U.N. development organizations. As a result, relations with NGOs have failed to develop in ways that could be mutually rewarding. Recently, both the UNDP and World Bank have shown an interest in developing better working relations with NGOs.[22] Among other things, the UNDP has now developed mechanisms which enable it to finance NGOs as implementing partners in development projects. Joint UNDP/NGO feasibility studies of ICARA II projects will be among the first tests of these mechanisms. These are welcome developments which should be continued. The U.N. system by no means has a monopoly on knowledge about the development needs of Africa, especially in the hinterlands, where most of Africa's refugees reside. NGOs are often the only outside presence in those areas, and often are more sensitive to the special needs of refugees and of rural Africans in heavily refugee populated regions.

Many individuals in the NGO sector take credit for having identified the need for better integration between refugee aid and development, and have applauded the international community's recognition of doing something about it at ICARA II. Moreover, NGOs have access to a reservoir of volunteers and professional talent that the U.N. system might otherwise be unable to tap. ICARA II provides an opportunity to explore ways in which NGO and U.N. agencies can work together to address refugee-related development needs. It is an opportunity that should not be lost.

Another potential problem in NGO/U.N. system efforts to coordinate their ICARA II response has to do in part with geography. Many of the most active NGOs in preparation for ICARA II are headquartered in Geneva. UNDP headquarters are, of course, in New York, and only a small office is maintained in Geneva. Yet the bulk of the 5c projects will be coordinated by UNDP. The already existing preference of many European NGOs and others that are headquartered in Geneva to work with the UNHCR instead of the UNDP could be reinforced if the UNDP does not make a special effort to reach out to this group of NGOs. The UNDP has the advantage of proximity in dealing with the large number of American NGOs headquartered in New York and Washington, D.C. But it would be unfortunate for the NGO sector to be divided by the Atlantic. The UNDP should make every effort to bridge this oceanic gap. Fortunately, there is some evidence of a growing European NGO willingness to entertain relationships with the UNDP.

As suggested above, the U.N. system can take a number of steps to improve the prospects for a successful response to ICARA II. But some factors are beyond its control. For instance, a deepening of the drought-induced African famine would severely hamper progress on ICARA II implementation. Indeed, the U.N. system has few resources it can bring directly to bear on ICARA II projects. Although the U.N. can facilitate donor response and try to promote ICARA II projects with the donors, it is the donor governments, themselves, that control the purse strings. In the end it matters little how well-oiled and efficient

U.N. coordination of ICARA II follow-up is, if there are insufficient resources to fund meritorious projects. For this reason, it is essential that we next examine the crucial role of donor countries respecting ICARA II and efforts to link refugee and development assistance.

NOTES

1. See U.N. General Assembly Resolution 20/2029, 22 November 1965, which established the UNDP. The General Asembly action was based on ECOSOC resolution 37/1020 of 11 August 1964 which had initially recommended the merger of existing development assistance programs into a single entity.
2. UNDP, *Annual Report of the Administrator for 1983*, (New York: June 1984), p. 10.
3. See *ibid.*, Basic Program data section, DP/1984/5/Add.3, p. 6 for data on contribution levels.
4. See A/39/402/Add.1, p. 5.
5. See *ibid.*, for a more detailed description of specific ICARA II follow-up unit responsibilities.
6. *Ibid.*, p. 5.
7. See A/CONF125/2, pp. 24–25 for official description of finance mechanisms.
8. See *supra*, Chapter 2, note 7.
9. The Constitution of the IRO was concluded on 15 December 1946 in New York and entered into force on 20 August 1948. The Statute of the Office of the UNHCR was established on 14 December 1950 by U.N. General Assembly resolution 5/428. The U.N. Convention Relating to the Status of Refugees was subsequently concluded on 28 July 1951 in Geneva and entered into force on 22 April 1954. For a thorough study of the origins and work of the IRO and UNHCR see; Louise Holborn, *The International Refugee Organization. A Specialized Agency of the United Nations: Its History and Work, 1946–1952.* (London: Oxford University Press, 1956); and, Idem., *Refugees: A Problem of Our Time, The Work of the United Nations High Commissioner for Refugees, 1951–1972.* 2 vols, (Metuchen: Scarecrow Press, 1975).
10. For a readable description of UNHCR refugee settlement activities in Africa, see; UNHCR, *Special Report: Refugee Integration: A New Start* (Geneva: UNHCR Public Information Section), especially at pp. 9, 15, and 16–17.
11. The World Bank project in Pakistan is a classic example of how UNHCR has played such a catalytic role.
12. See UNHCR Executive Committee, 34th Session, *Refugee Aid and Development* A/AC96/645, 28 August 1984.

13. *Ibid.,* pp. 6 & 9.
14. See the World Bank statement to ICARA II, July 1984 for details on Bank views about its role in refugee-related development assistance.
15. See the WFP statement to ICARA II, July 1984.
16. For a compendium of press articles see, *ICARA II: From the Press* (Geneva: UNHCR, 1984).
17. See the 17 December 1984 statement by the Secretary-General on the Drought Situation in Africa.
18. See, for instance, Chiang Pei-heng. *Non-Governmental Organizations at the United Nations: Identity, Role, Function* (New York: Praeger Publishers, 1981).
19. NGLS services several U.N. agencies including, among others, the UNDP, UNICEF, FAO and the World Bank.
20. Angus Archer, 'Methods of Multilateral Management: The Interrelationship of International Organizations and NGOs', in Toby T. Gati, ed., *The United States, the United Nations, and the Management of Global Change* (New York: New York University Press, 1983), p. 321.
21. Ernst Gohlert, 'The Advisory Committee on Voluntary Foreign Aid and the Non-governmental Liaison Service: A Case Study in Organisation and Development', paper presented at the International Studies Association Meetings, Washington, D.C., March 1984, pp. 11–12 & 14.
22. Both organizations have undertaken internal reviews on how to deal with the NGO sector. This has been given added incentive by ICARA II, particularly in the case of the UNDP. An NGO/World Bank Committee was formed in 1984, to explore expanding their relationship. This committee is co-chaired by Mr. Kozlowski of ICVA and Mr. Burki of the Bank.

CHAPTER 4

Donor Country Response to ICARA II

The success of ICARA II hinges on the careful coordination of existing refugee and development agencies and the mobilization of resources to meet the refugee-related development needs of African countries. We saw in the last chapter that the U.N. system has taken several key steps to tackle the coordination issue. But coordination alone is not enough. Without the mobilization of a modest level of additional resources, ICARA II will be perceived at most as a half success. The degree of success achieved will depend to a large extent on the generosity of the donor countries.

In this chapter donor country attitudes about ICARA II and the linkage of refugee aid and development assistance, will be examined. This will be followed by a discussion of the general constraints facing donor country response, the actual response of donors since ICARA II and a comparative analysis of the constraints they have experienced in responding more aggressively.

DONOR COUNTRY ATTITUDES

In general, donor country attitudes toward ICARA II were marked initially by a lack of enthusiasm and in some cases outright circumspection. Most donors doubted the motives for the convening of ICARA II. As a rule, they felt – in contrast to the Africans – that ICARA I had been a success, and many were upset with the African criticism of their response to the first conference. Nevertheless, most donors determined that they would participate at ICARA II, wait and see what direction the conference would take, and make the best of it so that all con-

68

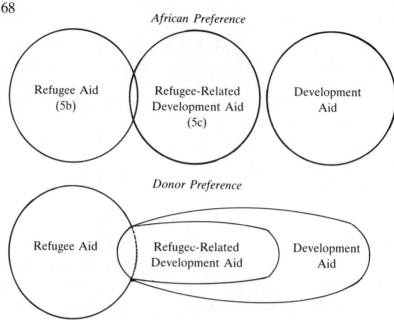

Figure 4.1. The relationship between international refugee and development assistance: African and donor preferences.

cerned would view it – unlike its predecessor ICARA I – as a success.

It was inevitable that basic differences would arise between the Africans and donor countries about how the concept of refugee-related development assistance should be operationalized. The differences centered around the desired relationship between refugee aid, development aid, and refugee-related development aid. The third category of assistance, was the *raison d'etre* of ICARA II. How should this new window of assistance relate to the traditional areas of refugee and development assistance? Figure 4.1 illustrates the different perspectives of the Africans and donors on this score.

Clearly not all African or donor country views on the relationship of refugee and development aid can be fitted neatly into the two different models presented in Figure 4.1. But there is little doubt that the models reflect the general thrust of African and donor country thinking. The Africans supported the idea of a separate and distinct 5c category of aid because it would be easier under those circumstances to determine whether the resources provided were additional to regular development assistance. The donors, on the other hand, conceived of the 5c project assistance as overlapping with the traditional refugee and development assistance categories. Most of them preferred, in other words, an integrated rather than a two track development aid system. Refugee-related development needs would be factored into the regular development planning process. Under this system additionality would be more difficult to determine.

Negotiations on the text of the ICARA II Final Declaration and Programme of Action reflected the different positions of the Africans and donors on the issues of additionality and the relationship between 5c activities and regular development programming. The upshot was a compromise in which both sides agreed on the need for both additionality and coordination of development and refugee planning. Whether this compromise can be effected in practical terms remains to be seen. Nearly two years after ICARA II, very little additional money has been provided by donors, and coordination of 5c and development programming activities on a country-by-country basis has gotten off to a slow start.[1] In the final analysis, the donors sit in the key position as far as determining the success of ICARA II follow-up. It is they who could stimulate the process by committing resources. However, they face a number of constraints which are detailed below.

DONOR COUNTRY CONSTRAINTS

Although the exact circumstances of each donor country vary, three general areas of constraint face them all. These include budgetary constraints, bureaucratic/organizational constraints and difficulties with inter-donor coordination.

Budgetary Constraints

One of the complaints made by many donor countries before ICARA II was that availability of additional foreign development assistance would be very limited. The global economy was still affected by recession, interest rates were high, and budget deficits continued to rise. Under such circumstances, legislatures were more concerned about trimming budgets than finding new ways to spend additional resources. Indeed, planners for ICARA II were keenly aware of these general constraints. The requests placed before ICARA II, which translated to about $100 million per year for four years, took into account the very real constraints that many donors faced. However, even these rather modest requests for additional resources would face tough going as donors weighed the relative merits of refugee-related development assistance against other budget priorities. In the months following ICARA II, the drought-related emergency needs in Africa had a further chilling effect on the availability of funds that might otherwise have been appropriated for use on ICARA II projects.

The budgetary constraint problem is further complicated in the non-parliamentary governments, most notably the United States, where executive/legislative relations must be taken into account in the budget process. Different substantive interests and budgetary priorities exist within each branch of government as well as between them. Some agencies are more attuned to and sympathetic with Africa's refugee-related development needs; others are more concerned about stemming the increase of budgetary outlays. In short, the budgetary process is fraught with potential obstacles or pitfalls for new budgetary requests. They can be killed easily at one stage only to be restored at another. But during a period of budgetary retrenchment, new requests for low priority items are extremely vulnerable to the budgetary scalpel, and, once excised, are more difficult to resurrect, as the U.S. case demonstrates so clearly.

Refugee Agency/Development Agency Relations

Whether or not they provide large amounts of additional resources, donors will need to consider mechanisms to coordinate their refugee and development agencies' activities. As we have noted before, ICARA II 5c projects fall into a borderline area between the traditional refugee aid and development assistance categories. They do not constitute a form of direct assistance to refugees, although some refugees may benefit from them. Nor do they necessarily fit into the long-term development plans of the host state or major development assistance donors. They are neither pure development nor pure refugee assistance, but rather a hybrid of the two. This raises the question of which agency within donor countries should assume major responsibility for 5c activities, the refugee or development agency, or both? The answer to this question of bureaucratic responsibility varies with each donor. The answer is even more complicated when different agencies have different priorities or where one agency must take responsibility for seeking the resources and another for administering them.

Problems with interaction between different government agencies are compounded even further when one considers differences that may arise between agency headquarters and its field operations. Even where a clear line of responsibility for ICARA II projects is established, these headquarter/field relations can be problematical. For instance, field offices may have little background or interest in refugee-related development projects. In addition many of the ICARA II projects call for 'fast money' which would be expended over a period of a few years. Field people generally conceive of development projects as lasting for much longer periods of time. They may be reluctant to take on smaller, less well-integrated projects that may be outside their main developmental or geographical focus, or that may overburden their personnel capacities. For these reasons, donor governments must necessarily consider the constraints on implementation capabilities of their field staff, and where appropriate devise approaches to overcome them.

Donor Country Interaction

A final constraint on donor country response to ICARA II centers on donor interaction with each other. To a certain extent, the UNDP will perform a clearinghouse function which will allow donors to stay abreast of their various ICARA II activities. However, direct communications between governments also will be useful where they have interests in the same countries and project sectors.

Prior to ICARA II, donors shared information frequently on their evaluations of project concepts through the sub-group of the WHLG on ICARA II. Since ICARA II some consultation between donors has continued, but it has lagged considerably in comparison to the pre-conference period. Unless donors continue to consult on a regular basis, ICARA II will begin to lose visibility, and the possibilities for wasted energy on duplicative projects will increase.

All donors in one way or another face budgetary and organizational constraints. Still, in the months immediately following ICARA II, several of the donors quickly undertook technical reviews and funded projects. This momentum lost steam in the fall of 1984 as the enormity of the drought and famine in Africa began to occupy time and energy. By the spring of 1985, some donors began to refocus on ICARA II after the initial shock of Africa's emergency needs passed. The modest renewal of interest was perhaps a result of the realization that future emergencies can be prevented or mitigated only if more attention is paid to infrastructural development such as that proposed by ICARA II.

Before we examine the specific problems faced by several of the key donors, it will be useful to recount what donors said they would do at ICARA II to address refugee-related burdens and what they have done since to follow through on promises made. Finally, several observations on the question of additionality will be offered along with suggestions about how donor countries could respond more effectively to ICARA II.

THE INITIAL DONOR RESPONSE TO ICARA II AND COMPARISONS TO ICARA I

Pinning down with precision the donor country response to ICARA II is a bit like trying to photograph a moving target. At one time donors express interest in particular projects based on a cursory reviews at headquarters, only to shy away after closer scrutiny.[2] In other cases more than one donor has shown interest in the same projects.[3] Some donors have indicated an interest in a large number of projects even though they could only fund a few of those mentioned.[4] Others have identified projects not in the ICARA II documentation but which have clear ICARA II implications.[5]

The difficulty in precisely determining what has been or is being done, is neither surprising nor undesirable. Development-related planning is always subject to flux as donor and recipient countries explore project opportunities. The ICARA II projects have been and should be no exception.

To trace the donor response, it is useful to begin with the announcements of support made at ICARA II. Table 4.1 lists the amounts either pledged or mentioned by donors in support of 5b, 5c or unspecified activities. It should be noted, however, that the amounts listed by no means necessarily represent additional funds.

The initial sums generated at ICARA II, itself, appear paltry in comparison to those raised at ICARA I. A comparison of Tables 4.1 and 4.2 shows that ICARA I raised about $ 567 million while ICARA II, at least initially, raised less than $ 90 million. Before one jumps to the conclusion that the donors have been laggard in response to ICARA II as compared to ICARA I, several points should be emphasized. First, ICARA I was a pledging conference while ICARA II was billed as a nonpledging one. Second, at ICARA I donors focused their attention primarily on the emergency needs of refugees which at that time were rather substantial, whereas the focus of ICARA II was on development-related needs. Third, the entire UNHCR Program for Africa in 1981 had been included in the ICARA I requests. At ICARA II, the regular program was not included in the requests made, rather, only additional needs were included in the actual requests. Fourth, although $ 567 million were pledged at ICARA I, considerably less than $ 500 million was actually contributed. Moreover, much of it was spent over a three year period and only a modest proportion, perhaps half of the total, represented truly additional funds.[6] Nevertheless, the money generated, whether new or old, was equal to the task of addressing the emergency needs and later the care and maintenance needs of the refugees. The point is that ICARA I and ICARA II cannot be fairly compared on the basis of funds generated alone. Indeed, ICARA II was seen by the donors as an opportunity to build principles on refugee-related development assistance which had been ignored at ICARA I for numerous reasons that we have already reviewed.

Still there are striking differences between the financial bottom lines of the two conferences. For instance, the United States ($ 283 million), the EC ($ 68 million) and the FRG ($ 43 million)

74

Table 4.1. Pledges made at ICARA II (in thousands of US$).

Donor country	5b activities	5c activities	Unspecified
Australia	1,734		
Austria	128	4,960	
Bahrain			20
Canada	1,200	10,540	
China			1,000[a]
Denmark	1,171	3,000	
Finland		10,000	
France		890	
FRG	1,964		
Holy See		300	
Indonesia			20[b]
Ireland	82		
Italy		15,000	
Japan	6,000		
Kampuchea			1
Kenya	21		
Korea	20		
Malawi	4		
Malaysia			10[c]
Netherlands	2,000		
New Zealand	95		
Norway	1,887	2,000	
Oman			100
Saudi Arabia			5,000[d]
Singapore			10
Spain		250	
Sweden	1,829	3,000	
Switzerland	427		
Syria			10
Thailand			10
Tunisia			10
Turkey	10		
UK		5,000	
Yugoslavia			325[e]
Total	18,563	54,940	6,516[f]

[a] Available for 5b and 5c.
[b] Specified for 5c after ICARA II.
[c] Specified for 5b after ICARA II.
[d] Specified for UNDP 5c Trust fund after ICARA II.
[e] In-kind contribution for humanitarian relief.
[f] Excludes a $50,000 donation by the U.N. Staff Council.

Table 4.2. Pledges made at ICARA I (in US$ as of June 1981).

Country	Amount
Algeria	300,000
Argentina	500,000
Australia	11,627,906
Belgium	2,492,754
Canada	18,823,529
China	1,000,000
Cyprus	3,000
Denmark	9,090,909
Egypt	1,000,000
Finland	2,962,963
France	2,474,747
FRG	42,857,143
Ghana	50,000
Iceland	10,000
India	10,000
Indonesia	20,000
Israel	300,000
Italy	17,000,000
Japan	33,000,000
Kampuchea (Democratic)	1,000
Lesotho	2,597
Liechtenstein	20,000
Luxembourg	17,390
Malawi	5,882
Malyasia	30,000
Netherlands	9,698,276
New Zealand	186,916
Nigeria	3,000,000
Norway	3,055,555
Pakistan	44,000
Philippines	10,000
Republic of Korea	20,000
Saudi Arabia	30,000,000
Sierra Leone	100,000
Singapore	10,000
Spain	1,000,000
Sweden	6,493,509
Switzerland	2,356,020
Syria	10,000
Tanzania	12,500
Thailand	10,000
Trinidad and Tobogo	2,083
Tunisia	15,000
United Arab Emirates	2,000,000
United Kingdom	13,863,636
United States	283,400,000
Upper Volta	4,032
Yugoslavia	78,125
European Communities	68,000,000
Total	566,969,472

accounted for nearly five-sevenths of the entire ICARA I take. None of these made a monetary pledge at ICARA II, although since the conference the United States has funded several projects and the EC has included in its Lomé III agreement with the African, Carribean and Pacific (ACP) states, about $ 70 million which could be used for ICARA II-like projects over the next five years. By contrast Italy ($ 15 million) and Finland ($ 10 million) were the donors making the largest pledges at ICARA II.

Finally, in comparing ICARA I and II it is important to emphasize that ICARA II, unlike its predecessor, was conceptualized as one stage of a longer term process. Thus, although the bottom line of success no doubt will focus at least in part on the amount of resources eventually generated, final conclusions about the success of ICARA II should be deferred for several years. It is useful then to look not only at pledges made at ICARA II itself, but to examine donor expressions of interest in particular projects and countries. This may give us a better sense of the future prospects for ICARA II than focusing only on monetary pledges made at the conference.

DONOR ACTIVITY SINCE ICARA II

Donor expressions of interest in ICARA II projects varied considerably. Italy, France and Sweden, for instance, made pledges at ICARA II but did not specify which projects they might fund. Some indicated only which countries' submissions were being studied. On the other hand, a number of donors, including the Netherlands, Japan and the United States, made no 5c pledges, but expressed interest in specific projects or general interest in certain countries or sectoral areas. Table 4.3 shows donor expressions of interest made at or since ICARA II in 5c projects or host countries. It should not be interpreted as a definitive summary of which projects or how many of them will be funded. Rather, it depicts how many projects and which countries have been under study by donors. The table illustrates that most of the recipient countries are receiving a fair amount of donor interest. The conspicuous exceptions are Uganda (with only one project under consideration) and Swaziland (with none, excepting a UNHCR-

Table 4.3. Expressions of interest in ICARA II 5c projects countries.

Host countries

Donors	Angola	Bots-wana	Burundi	Ethiopia	Kenya	Lesotho	Rwanda	Somalia	Sudan	Swazi-land	Uganda	Tanza-nia	Zaire	Zambia
Argentina									1				2	
Austria				1								*		
Belgium			*					1			1			
Canada		2		1			1		2			2	1	1
Denmark		1			1							*		
EC	1			*				*	*					
Egypt				*										
Finland								1	1					
France	*		*	*	1		*	2						1
FRG					1				5					2
Holy See							1							
Ireland						*						*		*
Italy	*			*				*	1					*
Japan								*	2			*	*	*
Netherlands		1					3	1	5			3	1	1
Norway		2			1				2			1		
Portugal	1													
Sweden	*	*		*	*	*						*		*
Switzerland				2	*				2			*		*
UK	*	*		*	*	1		*	*		*			
USA	*	*			1	1	2	*	2		1		3	1
Yugoslavia									1					

Numerals indicate the number of host country projects which have been specifically identified by donors for study and/or implementation.
* Indicates countries in which donors have expressed interest but have not identified specific projects.

NOTE: Table does not include countries submitting proposals after ICARA II (i.e., Cameroon, Central African Republic, Chad, Djibouti and Guinea). Brazil, Chile and Greece indicated at ICARA II that they were studying the documentation. Australia stated that it would be in contact with UNDP. Other donors (Saudi Arabia, China, and Indonesia) have contributed resources directly to the UNDP Trust Fund without specifying countries or projects of interest.

funded project). Not included in the table are those five African countries which submitted proposals after ICARA II. Donors have yet to show a great deal of interest in these countries. On the whole, however, it is fair to say that donors have conducted follow-up studies on over half of the 128 5c projects initially placed before ICARA II.

While the studies continue, actual progress on implementation of projects has been very slow. As of February 1986, only nine ICARA II or ICARA II-related projects actually have received funding and were under implementation (see Table 4.4). On the other hand, the thirty-six projects listed in Table 4.4 have received donor commitments for full or in some cases partial funding. The Netherlands and the United States were among the first to begin implementation of projects despite the fact that neither made a pledge at ICARA II. The projects they have funded are listed in Table 4.4.

They are not alone, however. Several other donors quickly fielded teams to conduct feasibility studies on ICARA II projects. The Italian government sent missions to Sudan and Somalia and tried unsuccessfully to mount a mission to Ethiopia – the latter was postponed because relevant Ethiopian ministries were unable to prepare for it owing to the overwhelming pressures created by the drought emergency. Japan, Finland, Norway and Canada also have fielded ICARA II technical missions to one or more African countries, and several other donors including Austria, Switzerland, the United States and the Netherlands have entered into negotiations on particular projects.

The reaction of donor countries since ICARA II suggests that they are interested in responding to refugee-related development needs. After a period of inactivity on ICARA II – a period corresponding to the initial months in which response to the drought emergency was of a far higher priority – donor activity on ICARA II began to percolate once again in the spring of 1985. Momentum on a number of projects was regained and the EC moved decisively into the picture with a substantial financial commitment. While only modest amounts of additional resources have been made available thus far, some donors have sought conscientiously to apply them and other existing resources to ICARA II needs. In so doing, they have faced several constraints which we will be examined below.

Table 4.4. ICARA II projects with confirmed funding.

Recipient	Donor	Project
Angola	EEC	Uige Agricultural Extension
Botswana	Canada	Poultry Raising/Marketing
	Canada	Dukwe Health Screening
	Norway	Dukwe Reafforestation
Djibouti	UNDP/WHO	Dikhil Tuberculosis Control
	UNDP	Balbala Health Care Center
Ethiopia	Austria/Italy	Health Infrastructure
	Italy	Dire Dawa/Jijiga Food Storage
	Finland	Itang Food Storage (5b)
Kenya	Norwegian Refugee Council	Thika Vocational Training Center
Lesotho	UNDP	Health Centers
Rwanda	France	Reintegration of Returnees
	Holy See	Craft Train Center[a]
	USA	Nasho Cattle Ranch[a]
	USA[b]	Reafforestation[a]
Somalia	Italy/Yugoslavia	Health Clinics
	Finland	Grain Storage Warehouses[a]
	FRG	Northwest Reafforestation
	Italy	Port Handling Equipment
	Japan	Shabelli Water Development
	UNDP/UNHCS	Low Cost Housing[a]
Sudan	Japan	Kassala Water Supply
	Japan	Food Transportation
	Italy	Kassala Workshop
	Switzerland	Suakin Town Water Supply
	Switzerland	Port Sudan Water Supply
	UK[b]	Port Sudan Primary Education
	UK[b]	Agriculture Mechanization
	USA[b]	Gedaref Water[a]
Tanzania	Netherlands	Mpanda/Urambo Health Services
	Netherlands	Rural Development Centers
Zaire	Netherlands/USA	Aru/Shaba Health Project[a]
	USA	Shaba Water
	USA	Lualaba/Shaba Road Construction
Zambia	Egypt	Health Facilities
	USA	Aquaculture Development[a]

[a] Projects currently under implementation.
[b] Projects not included in the original ICARA II documentation, but which meet ICARA II 5c objectives.

Source: UNGA Document A/40/435, 16 July 1985, Report of the Secretary General on Assistance to Refugees in Africa.

ASSESSING THE CONSTRAINTS

The two key donor country constraints include budgetary limits and organizational/administrative difficulties surrounding relations between refugee/multilateral and development/bilateral agencies. Another problem facing donor countries as a group concerns their ability to coordinate their various ICARA II responses – an issue to which we will return later. For now we will focus on how several donors have coped with the budgetary and organizational difficulties. The cases examined below do not constitute an exhaustive list of all donor countries. They are the cases with which the author is most familiar. In addition, they help to illustrate how donors of varying sizes and with different political leanings and administrative approaches have coped with budgetary and organizational realities.

Evaluating the U.S. Case[7]

The U.S. government is the single largest contributor to the voluntary programs of the UNHCR. It contributes about 30 percent of the total budget for the UNHCR program on African refugees.[8] Additional resources are contributed through other international organizations and through bilateral channels. At ICARA I the United States announced a pledge of $283 million which was about half of the total amount pledged there.[9] The bulk of this pledge was for emergency assistance. But the United States eventually funded two ICARA I development-related refugee projects, one in Burundi and one in Swaziland. In addition, since ICARA I, about $45 million in bilateral resources have been channelled by the U.S. government through its African Resettlemment Services and Facilities Program (ARSFP) which was initiated in 1982. These resources have focused on refugee self-reliance activities as well as refugee-related development assistance in such infrastructure support activities as water development and reforestation.

In short, the U.S. government has a solid record in support of both emergency and development-related African refugee programs. Thus, even though it viewed the conference with circumspection, and took its time before announcing its intention to participate, the Africans had every expectation that the United States would respond favorably to the needs defined by ICARA II. However, budgetary and organizational constraints have limited the U.S. government's ability to respond as forthrightly and generously as might have been expected. Before exploring the constraints it will be useful to recount the U.S. government's basic attitudes toward the ICARA II process.

In part because the U.S. government felt that Africa's refugee needs were being met through existing multilateral and bilateral efforts, it did not believe initially that ICARA II was necessary. Its reservations were announced when the General Assembly voted in favor of resolution 37/197. Unlike many other donors, the United States remained silent on the question of whether it would attend the conference. The other donors, many of whom shared U.S. skepticism, nevertheless determined early on that they would participate. But the U.S. government remained very noncommittal, until a decision was reached in February 1984 – only five months before the conference – that participation would serve U.S. interests.[10]

The inclusion of the UNDP in the ICARA II Steering Committee and the systematic and realistic preparation exhibited by ICARA II planners were important factors in paving the way for U.S. attendance. Still, U.S. attendance at ICARA II was predicated on the assumption that it would be a non-pledging conference.

At first, little thought was given as to how a nonpledging format could be operationalized in a way that would satisfy African country desires to see additional resources made available at ICARA II. But it was a realistic concept from the U.S. government standpoint insofar as only about $20 million of existing monies (mostly in the ARSFP), could be made readily available. No specific resources for ICARA II had been requested in the U.S. government's 1984 and 1985 budgets largely because of the noncommittal U.S. posture on attendance at the time those budgets were being prepared. This posture could not have been maintained credibly if requests for ICARA II had been made then. In addition, ICARA II's emphasis on development-related projects suggested that more scrutiny of potential projects was required than would be normally the case for straight refugee projects. Furthermore, donors received the final conference documentation in March 1984, and could hardly have been expected to conduct necessary feasibility studies by the July meeting. The argument advanced was that one could not pledge resources for projects that would clearly require further study and possibly redesign.

Instead, the United States argued strongly that ICARA II should be viewed as one stage in a longer term process of treating refugee-related development needs, rather than a one-shot pledging conference. Despite the nonpledging stance, it was prudent to begin serious review of the technical team reports in order to identify those projects in which the United States might have a potential interest. Some friction developed within the State Department over whether the process of review itself might subvert the nonpledging stance and lead to undesirable budgetary committments.[11] But the review continued. And for good reason: if the U.S. government were to arrive at ICARA II without having some tangible evidence of its intention to take the conference's projects seriously, then the going for the U.S. delegation would be rocky indeed. Africans might question why the United States even decided to attend.

The U.S. government arrived at ICARA II hoping that the limited amounts of non-additional resources that might be eventually made available under the ARSFP, along with a solemn promise that it would continue as it had in the past to alleviate the refugee burden, would satisfy the Africans. Still, some American officials felt that a more tangible expression of U.S. support might be necessary to back up the U.S. verbal commitment to a process that would alleviate refugee-related burdens.

Last minute efforts to explore possible budgetary strategies that would allow the U.S. government to speak more forcefully about its intentions to address seriously Africa's refugee-related developments burdens, were marked by renewal of lingering tensions between the principal agencies responsible for U.S. refugee and development planning, that is State/RP and AID. The problem boiled down to this: which of the two agencies would be willing, even hypothetically, to request funds for ICARA II, either in a supplemental to its 1985 budget or as requests in subsequent annual budgets. In a nutshell, AID, which in principle ought to have taken the lead given the clear development focus of most of the 5c projects, instead demurred. Hence, State/RP concluded that it would have to seek resources in its 1986 budget so that the U.S. government would be in a position to follow through on the verbal commitments it would make at ICARA II.

AID reluctance to take the lead on ICARA II requires explanation – especially since the United States had stated consistently that efforts to link refugee and development assistance would require greater coordination between refugee and development agencies both at the host country and the international level. Presumably this should apply to donor countries as well. To what extent has the U.S. government lived up to its own advice on this score?

In fact there has been a fair degree of coordination between RP and AID in dealing with refugee-related development questions in Africa. Projects implemented under the ARSFP have required joint RP/AID programming. In addition, RP called on AID Missions to review ICARA II projects. But there is also a basic difference in orientation and focus between the two agencies, which flows from their respective mandates and legislative authorities.[12] Stated simply, RP handles refugee assistance and AID handles development assistance. But refugee-related development assistance falls between this simplistic and traditional division of labor. Whose responsibility really is it? The possibilities are three: that it should belong exclusively to either AID or RP, or that it should be shared by them. As we will see shortly the first two options have not been suitable on the one hand because of a lack of institutional inclination on the part of AID on the other because of a lack of institutional expertise on the part of RP. As a result, the answer given in the past, as reflected in the operation of the ARSFP, has been that it is a shared responsibility. In fact, this is probably the most appropriate answer, but it does not solve the problem of *how* the responsibility will be shared and whether the two agencies really want to share it.

AID Administrator, Peter McPherson, for instance, has made no secret of the fact that refugee assistance to Africa should be administered by AID, arguing – not without some justification – that most African refugee situations are really now long-term development ones. For obvious reasons, RP officials have not been enthusiastic supporters of this idea. But, perhaps even more importantly, neither have been most of the working level people in AID many of whom do not view refugee-related projects as a truly mainstream development activity. Refugee projects are often perceived as a sideshow and in some cases as irrelevant to the development strategy of the host country. Although not everyone in AID shares these somewhat skeptical views of refugee-related projects, only a few would instinctively initiate such projects as a regular part of their development programming and others would actively resist efforts to do so. This lack of institutional enthusiasm for refugee-related development projects in AID was reflected in its somewhat lethargic response to preparation for ICARA II.

While resisting the argument that all refugee assistance ought to be administered by AID, RP recognized nonetheless that it did not possess the requisite expertise to assess and implement fully the largely developmental projects being considered by ICARA II. This combination of AID hesitation to take an active role and the turf sensitivities between the two agencies did not foster a high degree of coordination and cooperation in planning for ICARA II.

Despite the difficulties that arose in coordinating ICARA II assistance, the United States was able to act quickly after the conference to fund a number of projects. Sufficient groundwork had been done to allow obligation of the remainder of the resources in the ARSFP account toward funding of ICARA II projects in Zaire and Rwanda. These projects coupled with add-on funding to ongoing ICARA-like projects in Sudan and Chad totalled about $17.5 million.[13] None of this represented additional money, but it was evidence of the U.S. desire to respond favorably to ICARA II. Once this money was spent, however, there was little left in U.S. coffers.

An analysis of how much the U.S. government should be prepared to contribute toward ICARA II projects is a necessarily tentative exercise. Still some general observations can be made. Taking the $430 million in requests made at or shortly after ICARA II, and assuming that at least $50 million of this is for projects that are already dated or without merit, one is left with a figure of about $380 million. The U.S. government has traditionally contributed about one-quarter to a third of the UNHCR regular program for Africa. Assuming a one-quarter level contribution to ICARA II, this would amount to about $95 million spread out over three years – or a little more than $30 million per year. Some of this – perhaps as much as a third – could be met through existing resources or through reprogramming future resources. The other $60 million would have to come from additional appropriations.

However, for reasons that have been noted above, no money had been requested by the executive branch for ICARA II in its 1984 and 1985 budgets. Nor had a budget-conscious Congress been ready to appropriate such funds. RP had determined after considerable study that a request for ICARA II money in the 1985 supplemental would not survive the Office of Management and Budget's (OMB) scrutiny.

Attention turned within the Executive branch toward what could be done to secure resources for ICARA II in the 1986 budget. RP believed that AID should take lead responsibility given the development focus of the ICARA II projects and AID's expertise in programming such activities, but AID refused, suggesting that it was not interested in requesting additional resources at a time when Reagan's budget deficits were mounting. AID was skeptical that such a request would survive OMB budget axe. It would accept any Congressional appropriation for ICARA II in its budget, but refused to request any funds, despite some sentiment within its Africa Bureau to do so.

Under these circumstances, it was up to RP to take the lead. Otherwise, momentum on follow-through to U.S. commitments would be lost, perhaps irretrievably. In rationalizing its 1986 budget request, RP determined that, while it did not have adequate staffing to program the large amount of resources involved, it could nevertheless act as a conduit for them. In other words, it could channel resources on a case-by-case basis through the UNDP, other U.N. agencies, NGOs, or, where there was specific interest expressed, through AID Missions. Based on these assumptions, RP sought $25 million for ICARA II in the regular 1986 State Department request.

As if in fulfillment of the AID prophecy, OMB cut the ICARA II line out of RP's 1986 budget request. RP then approached AID once again to see how resources might be made available in 1986. The upshot was an agreement by AID to review its regular development program to see whether resources could be re-programmed for ICARA II. But there were two problems with this. First, such funds would not be additional and hence would fall short of satisfying African expectations. Second, it was un-likely that much money could be milked from a reprogramming exercise. In short, ICARA II was mired down in the budgetary politics of the Executive Branch.

In the meantime, the U.S. Congress took up the question of ICARA II funding. In September 1984, an emergency supple-mental bill was introduced in the House by Representatives Weiss and Wolpe.[14] In addition to substantial food assistance to meet drought-related needs in Africa, the bill initially included $ 50 million for ICARA II. A revised version of this bill was re-introduced in January 1985. At the suggestion of private agencies, half of the proposed $ 50 million for ICARA II were earmarked for the UNDP Trust fund in order to maximize the available programming capabilities of U.S. agencies and to underscore stated U.S. support for the UNDP as the lead ICARA II agency.[15]

However, objections were raised in the House Appropriations Committee regarding the inclusion of development resources, including those for ICARA II in the bill. For the most part, these were cut from the bill or tied more explicitly to the emergency. The House voted out a final version which appropriated $ 12.5 million, only some of which could be used exceptionally for ICARA II, where the projects had a connection with emergency needs.[16] Language calling for contributions through the UNDP Trust Fund was also deleted. The House argued that the Execu-tive branch had a duty to address the longer-term needs of Africa – such as those dealt with by ICARA II – in its 1986 budget request.[17] But as we have seen, OMB had already seen to it that no request for ICARA II would be made in the 1986 budget. To make matters even worse, that portion of the supplemental that authorized appropriations for disaster and refugee assistance was made hostage to the American farm relief bill, which President Reagan vetoed in March 1985. The President stated, however, that he would consider an authorization for disaster and refugee assistance as part of an overall appropriations bill.

The House and Senate went back to work drafting supplemental legislation. By 21 March, both Houses had agreed to legislation authorizing a ceiling on non-food aid, including $ 37.5 million for refugee assistance.[18] Up to 54 percent of any funds appropriated under this authorization could be made available to the U.N. Office of Emergency Operations in Africa (UNOEOA) for 'projects such as those proposed at ICARA II'. However, the appropriations bill (H.R. 1239) earmarked $ 25 of the $ 37.5 million for replenishment of the President's world wide Emergency Refugee and Migration Assistance Fund, leaving only $ 12.5 million which could be used for ICARA II.[19] Because the 54 percent criterion could be applied only against the $ 12.5 million, a maximum of only $ 6.75 million could be spent on ICARA II-related projects. This legislation was reported out of a House/Senate conference on 27 March 1985, and was signed into law by the President on 4 April 1985. Unfortunately, little of the $ 6.75 million has since been spent on ICARA II, mainly because of the more pressing emergency needs. Also, OMB argued that while the supplemental permitted use of resources for ICARA II, it did not require it. Hence, OMB has permitted expenditures only for emergency needs, leaving ICARA II utterly wanting for attention.

The fragmentation of the U.S. budget process resulted in a less than satisfactory response to ICARA II. Executive/legislative differences and inter-agency relations in the Executive branch have come into play. The least constructive player has been OMB. Had it allowed the State Department's $ 25 million request for 1986 to go forward, some momentum in the U.S. response to ICARA II could have been maintained. Instead, it chose to eliminate not only the State/RP request but also any other resources that might have been transferred from other State department Bureaus to RP for ICARA II purposes. OMB argued that requests for this purpose should be made by AID. But AID, as we have seen, and as OMB fully understood, had decided not to request any new resources for ICARA II. Moreover, when Congress has appropriated resources, OMB has prevented them from being channelled into ICARA II projects. The upshot is that the U.S. response to ICARA II has been greatly weakened.

Officially speaking, the U.S. government recognized at ICARA II the existence of refugee-related development burdens and the need to link projects aimed at meeting these burdens with regular development programming.[20] It joined in the consensus on the Final Declaration and Programme of Action which underscored these principles. It cited examples of ongoing U.S. ICARA II-related projects, and although it did not make a monetary pledge, promised to consider additional projects as resources became available. Accordingly, it would seem that the U.S. government has a responsibility, not to mention a political stake, in following through with these commitments. Indeed, some U.S. government agencies recognize that U.S. interests are served by following through on promises made at ICARA II. But there are countervailing forces – emanating mainly from OMB – and a host of practical problems which have confounded well-intentioned efforts to respond forthrightly. The problems need be only briefly recounted here.

First, it is necessary to consider the general context. ICARA II simply is not among the highest priorities in Washington. To the extent it might have received attention, it has been overshadowed by the admittedly more pressing emergency needs of Africa. Advocates of ICARA II were fighting an uphill battle even before the drought overwhelmed public attention. Their task has been complicated even further since. ICARA II did not have high visibility in the American political agenda even before the emergency. It has even less now.

Second, and related to the issue of priorities, is the very real issue of budget constraints. Put simply, during a time of budgetary retrenchment, low priority and new budget requests simply are much more vulnerable to the budget knife.

Third, even if the amount of additional resources are limited, careful coordination between RP and AID is still necessary. It is not yet clear that the two agencies have a similar interest in pursuing ICARA II projects. As in the case of the U.N. system, an inclination/expertise dilemma exists. State RP has the inclination which AID lacks, but AID has a greater institutional capacity. However, as we noted earlier, RP can overcome its development programming weakness by using the UNDP as a resource to conduct feasibility and design studies and even to monitor implementation. They should establish appropriate financial mechanisms in the years to come so that refugee-related development programming can be facilitated. In the meantime RP and AID need to discuss their budgetary strategies in a spirit of cooperation, rather than in the climate of competition and suspicion that marked early deliberations between them on ICARA II funding requests.

To date the U.S. government's contribution to ICARA II has not been commensurate with its traditional level of contributions to African refugee programs. As a result, the success of ICARA II will rest even more heavily on other donors, many of which, as we shall see below, have faced constraints similar to those of the United States.

The United Kingdom

The UK response to ICARA II follow-up has benefitted from the existence of methods to finance refugee-related development projects. In response to appeals for assistance by the UNHCR for the World Bank project in Pakistan, arrangements were made between the multilateral desk in the British Foreign Office and the bilateral desk on Pakistan in the Overseas Development Administration (ODA) to make funds available for this project. In this case a decision was taken to include resources in the Pakistan bilateral program which could subsequently be channeled either bilaterally or through the multilateral desk to the UNHCR or World Bank.

In short, even before ICARA II the bilateral and multilateral offices had been in communication on how to handle refugee-related development resources. Arrangements for financing of ICARA II projects have been equally flexible and pragmatic. Most of British resources will be programmed on a bilateral basis with specific NGOs. But overall monitoring of ICARA II follow-up is the responsibility of the Refugee and Disaster Unit in ODA.

Like many of the other donors, the UK attitude toward ICARA II was a cautious one. It had not been pleased with the negative reaction of the Africans to ICARA I, which it saw as a success. Nevertheless, if ICARA II were to be held, the view of the UK was that every effort should be made to ensure that it could be viewed as a success by all. To that end serious discussions began in early 1984 in ODA and other elements of the Foreign

Office. The UK response to ICARA II was conditioned by several factors: (1) the desire for a successful outcome, (2) the belief that a nonpledging format was preferable, (3) the vocal lobbying of British NGOs in support of ICARA II, and (4) the existence of mechanisms within the British government to coordinate bilateral development assistance and multileral aid (e.g., to the UNHCR for refugees).

Eventually, the UK decided that its desires to see ICARA II succeed and to avoid making a pledge were incompatible. A few weeks before ICARA II, it was determined that a pledge of five million pounds would be made. But the UK did not specify officially at ICARA II either countries or projects of interest. Moreover, it was decided that the five million pounds would be channeled through British and international NGOs over the next five years. This decision was based in part on the very active and vocal lobbying role the British Refugee Council (BRC) – an umbrella agency for British NGOs – took on ICARA II. In addition, British officials believed that NGOs had the right kind of contact in refugee-affected areas to address development planning effectively.[21] A document setting forth the terms of reference and guidelines for the development of proposals was subsequently circulated among NGOs.[22] The initiative for presentation of proposals was left to the NGOs themselves, whose response to the ODA gesture has been slow. Many NGOs felt the requirements for obtaining ODA resources were unnecessarily complicated. Only three projects amounting to about $500,000 in value were funded in 1985, although several new proposals are under consideration. In order to facilitate NGO response, the UK may need to revise its expectations for documentation of projects and take a less passive approach toward promotion of ICARA II projects among NGOs. If those steps fail to attract sufficient NGO interest, the resources could always be channeled through United Nations agencies, the UNDP Trust Fund, or programmed jointly with other donors.

The Federal Republic of Germany

The FRG was one of four countries (the others were Belgium, Luxembourg, and the United States) that called for and abstained

on a separate vote on the operative paragraph of the UNGA
Third Committee resolution which called for the convening of
ICARA II.[23] The FRG later joined in the consensus on the
resolution as a whole, along with the other abstaining countries.
Still it had reservations about the need for ICARA II. Indeed,
like both the UK and the United States, the FRG had been a
pioneer in developing programs to address refugee-related development needs. A year before the U.N. vote on ICARA II, the
FRG began to explore ways to address these needs. Having
already taken substantial steps to tackle this problem, the FRG
wondered what more could be contributed by holding a conference. Still, it was prepared to use ICARA II as a forum to share
its own experience in the area of refugee-related development
assistance. Thus, although it made no monetary pledge, the FRG
did reaffirm its intention to continue reviewing ICARA II projects. It also cited the FRG's expenditure since 1983 of nearly $ 27
million on refugee-related programs in a variety of sectors
throughout the world.[24] This program will continue to be supported in the future and the FRG intends to spend about $ 15–20
million on it in the next few years. Indeed, it announced interest at
ICARA II in a total of ten projects in four countries (see Table
4.3).[25] Feasibility studies are planned for a project in Somalia and
possibly in Sudan.

The FRG's Ministry of Economic Cooperation has recognized
the validity of considering the refugee element in formulation of
its bilateral assistance program for some time. For example, after
ICARA I the FRG devised a water development program in a
refugee affected region of eastern Sudan. The UNHCR later sited
a camp in the project area. The FRG agreed to finance bilaterally
construction of wells, and other infrastructure, in and outside the
camp. After several delays in its bilateral efforts, the FRG decided to contribute some of the bilateral funds directly to the
UNHCR for development of the refugee water program. The
FRG and UNHCR effort proved to be a sensible, practical solution to integrate refugee and development aid. If the FRG had
insisted that bilateral funds could not be given to a multilateral
agency, this project might have been killed. Fortunately, the FRG
approached the problem flexibly and pragmatically. This formula
also has been applied by the FRG to the World Bank Project in

Pakistan, where it has contributed about $7 million of bilateral resources to the total $20 million package.[26]

ICARA II projects could be treated in a similar fashion. However, the FRG has indicated in this instance that most of the projects will be funded on a bilateral basis. The important point, however, is that the bilateral desks are aware of and attentive to the need to consider the refugee element in development planning. Moreover, there has been good collaboration between the Foreign Ministry and the Ministry of Economic Cooperation, and within the latter, among the various bilateral desks, technical offices, multilateral divisions and the planning unit for ICARA II. Indeed FRG officials point out that the refugee element is routinely considered as part of its regular development planning.

The FRG has approached several African countries of asylum about moving ICARA II projects into the context of its ongoing bilateral development programming. Several ICARA II projects continue to be under review in this context. However, because of budgetary constraints, actual funding for many of these projects may be delayed for quite some time, although a few are expected to be initiated shortly. In the meantime the preexisting Sudanese water project, which has clear ICARA II implications has been bolstered with additional aid. In Chad, Guinea and the Central African Republic, FRG officials note that their existing programs there overlap with many of the ICARA II projects submitted by these countries. In short, although the FRG has problems with the notion of additionality and formally made no pledge at ICARA II, it seems likely that it will continue to finance refugee-related development programs in Africa as it has in Pakistan and other countries for the last four years.

Italy[27]

Prior to 1979, Italy had not been an active donor in either humanitarian or development programs. Since then, it has become increasingly active in both areas, with the vast majority of resources now going to Africa. Indeed, about two-thirds of Italy's foreign assistance goes to countries in the Horn of Africa.

The government of Italy attaches great importance to the political and humanitarian aspects of the refugee problem in Africa. It has stated its belief that the African countries truly need assistance, that the refugee situation clearly aggravates an already deplorably low level of development, and that donors have a responsibility to help. Based on these tenets, Italy pledged $15 million at ICARA II, claiming that these were additional resources. Because this was the largest pledge made and because it was represented as an additional contribution, it was well-received by the Africans.

The Italian response since ICARA II has also been encouraging. Although Italy had made a significant pledge, it was not prepared to actually finance projects without first taking a close look at their feasibility. Immediately after ICARA II, it sent messages to several countries expressing its desire to field technical missions to review particular projects. Missions to Sudan and Somalia have since been accomplished, and several projects are in various stages of review in those countries and in Ethiopia prior to implementation.

Decisions on allocation of funds for refugee-related projects have been made in consultation between an emergency operations desk within the Foreign Ministry and the Department for Cooperation and Development. Actual monitoring of ICARA II follow-up until the spring of 1985 was handled through the emergency desk. However, in March 1985, the Italian parliament passed legislation which will create a full-fledged Department of Emergency Intervention. This new body will handle both refugee and other emergency assistance. It is still not clear whether the ICARA II projects will be monitored by this new department or the Department for Cooperation and Development. Experience suggests that great care should be taken by Italy to delineate the responsibilities between these two agencies respecting refugee-related development programs. Otherwise the rather smooth and unencumbered arrangements that previously existed for decision making on allocation of refugee and development resources could be replaced with a system affected by bureaucratic turf disputes.

Japan

Like many of the other donors, Japan had reservations about the need for ICARA II. It preferred a nonpledging format, and was concerned about the concept of additionality since its budgetary process for development-related projects precluded quick decisions about funding. Japanese wariness was overcome a month before the conference convened, based largely on its belief that contacts between the HLWG and the African group in Geneva had produced consensus about the purposes and nature of ICARA II. The Japanese Mission in Geneva was instrumental in fashioning its government's positive response to ICARA II. Although no large pledges were announced at the conference, Japan viewed it as a success because it was marked by a moderate approach, it avoided political polemics and because the Western group adopted a conciliatory approach toward African needs.

For Japan, the linkage of refugee aid and development poses some administrative problems, centering largely on where the money for such projects should come from and whether they should be handled through bilateral or miltilateral offices. Although all Japanese assistance is handled by the Overseas Economic Cooperation Bureau, there is a functional division between bilateral and multilateral assistance. Almost all of Japan's development assistance is done bilaterally by the Economic Cooperation Bureau (ECB). However, multilateral funds to agencies like the UNHCR and UNDP, are channeled through the U.N. Affairs Bureau. The infrastructural (5c) projects normally would be handled by the bilateral assistance side, but the refugee-related nature of such projects does not lend itself readily to the traditional development focus of the ECB. This has changed somewhat because of ICARA II, and the ECB has considered ways to promote the linkage of humanitarian/refugee aid with regular development programming.[28]

Despite the ECB's new awareness of the refugee element in development planning the process for implementation of ICARA II projects will be a long one. They are being treated in much the same way as regular development assistance, to wit: the Cabinet must give permission for bilateral projects once their feasibility has been established by the ECB and provided the Diet has voted sufficient funds. Japan is currently exploring the feasibility of ICARA II projects in the areas of water, health and agricultural development with five African host countries (Sudan, Somalia, Zaire, Zambia and Tanzania).[29] To that end, technical missions have been sent to these countries. However, Japan has indicated on several occasions that additionality will not apply to these projects. Rather, the Japanese believe that the refugee element must be integrated into the regular development programming.

Because Japan's ICARA II efforts will be funded on a bilateral basis, resources will be channeled through the Japan International Corporation Agency (JICA) or through local implementors in the host countries. Nevertheless, Japan recognizes the coordinating role of the UNDP on a country-by-country basis. In its view, this is necessary because the ultimate goal of ICARA II is to ensure complementarity between refugee-related programs and because UNDP has responsibility for coordination of U.N. development activities in Third World countries.

As a result of the tremendous humanitarian needs caused by the African drought, Japanese public awareness of African development and relief needs is greater today than at any time in the past.[30] The Japanese media have been more attuned to the problem and the government has initiated public awareness programs. In addition Japanese Foreign Minister Shintaro Abe, has made two trips to Africa, one with NGO representatives surveying the drought situation. In short, the possibility for active Japanese involvement in follow up to ICARA II seems very good despite the lack of readily available additional resources.

Finland and the Nordic Countries

Of all the Nordic countries, Finland's response to ICARA II has been the most vigorous. The other Nordic countries pledged money at ICARA II but in smaller amounts: Denmark about $2.7 million, Norway about $2 million and Sweden about $3 million. (Iceland made no pledge at ICARA II.) Finland pledged about $10 million – more than the other Nordic countries pledges combined. Indeed, Finland's pledge at ICARA II was second in size only to that of Italy.

Since ICARA II several of the Nordics have engaged in negotiation, with hosts on specific projects. Denmark has had bilateral discussions with Tanzania. Norway has funded Kenya's vocational training project with the YMCA and is reviewing a reforestation project in Botswana and school projects in Tanzania,

Sudan and Zambia. Sweden has expressed interest in projects improving water supply and agricultural production. As the country which first proposed that the UNHCR undertake a study of the linkages between refugee aid and development, Sweden has had a continuing interest in this subject. Prior to ICARA II it committed a sizable additional sum of money for ICARA II like projects in Angola, Botswana, and Zambia. Since ICARA II, however, resource availability has been a major constraint.[31]

While several of the Nordic countries have been active since ICARA II, project implementation has proceeded most quickly in Finland. In Sudan, for instance, Finland decided to extend an ongoing refugee-related infrastructural project involving agricultural equipment and training which was initially financed after ICARA I.[32] An additional $2 million is being spent on an extension of this project under ICARA II. In addition to this project which is already under implementation, the Finnish government sent technical missions to Ethiopia and Somalia in March 1985 to study food storage projects. Slightly less than $1 million will be used to build two food storage warehouses in the Gambela area of Ethiopia. This area was selected in consultation with the Ethiopian government after the Italians announced their intention to finance warehouses in Dire Dawa. The Finns had been interested in that site initially, but were willing to consider the suggested alternative.

The largest of the Finnish-sponsored ICARA II projects will be in Somalia, where $7 million have been alloted for 17 food storage warehouses to be interspersed throughout the four major areas in Somalia where there are large concentrations of refugees. A central warehouse also will be constructed in Mogadishu.

The forthright response of the Finnish government to ICARA II can be explained in part by the great importance it attaches not only to refugee and humanitarian aid but to development assistance as well.[33] Like the other donors, humanitarian and development assistance are administered by separate agencies; the former by the Political Department in the Foreign Ministry and the latter by Finnida. The two agencies have worked very closely since ICARA I to effect the agricultural project in Sudan. Money for this project originated in the Foreign Ministry and was transferred to Finnida which has monitored project implementation and supplemented the project with its own resources. The ICARA II projects will be funded primarily by Finnida, but the Political Department of the Foreign Ministry also has contributed about $1.2 million for 1986.[34] Refugee-related development assistance is a major priority for both agencies, which have found mutual collaboration to be a natural by-product of their similar views regarding the need for this kind of assistance. Although resource availability is a constraint in Finland as elsewhere, the Parliament nevertheless has been open to the use of resources for refugee-related development assistance. The overall budgets for refugee and development aid have increased only slightly (more for humanitarian than for development aid) which means that much of the ICARA II money will be financed from existing levels of resources. But insofar as Sudan, Ethiopia and Somalia are concerned, the resources will be additional to their ongoing development programs. They will be financed with funds that otherwise would have been invested in other countries.

The European Communities (EC)[35]

The EC, as noted earlier, had been a major contributor at ICARA I. At ICARA II, the EC made no pledge although it agreed with the basic principles enunciated at the conference. The primary reason no pledge was made was that the EC had no resources to commit. Negotiations on the Lomé III agreement were not to be completed until December of 1984, several months after ICARA II. Only then was the EC able to speak with authority on the level of financial resources that might be available for ICARA II.

EC attention to the linkage of refugee aid and development assistance was first highlighted in the Dury Report, which emphasized the need for intermediate aid to enhance refugee self-sufficiently and integration.[36] Following the Dury Report the EC included about 3 million European Currency Units (ECUs) in its 1985 budget to assist refugees in the post-emergency phase of subsistence. (EC emergency assistance to refugees is cut off after 6 months.) Still, these resources did not quite address the issue of refugee integration or the refugee's impact on the development infrastructure of host countries. But ICARA II was beginning to make an impact on EC thinking. Prior to Lomé III, there was really no intermediate mechanism to finance refugee-related development projects. The EC's budgetary capacities were limited to short-term emergency aid, long-term development assistance, and for the first time in 1984–85 some intermediate care and maintenance for refugees. But the projects proposed under the ICARA II 5c framework fell between existing aid mechanisms. This lacuna was filled by article 204 of the Lomé III agreement which states:

1. Aid may be granted to ACP States taking in refugees or returnees to meet acute needs not covered by the emergency aid, to implement in the longer term projects and action programmes aimed at self-sufficiency and the integration or reintegration of such people.
2. It shall be administered and implemented under procedures permitting rapid action. Conditions for payment and implementation shall be laid down case by case.
3. Such aid may be implemented, if the ACP State concerned so agrees, through an intermediary in conjuction with specialized organization, in particular the United Nations, or by the Commission direct.[37]

The EC interprets this article broadly to cover both the 5b and 5c elements of the ICARA II process. Moreover, the convention makes available 80 million ECU (about $70 million) for the years 1985–1990. Should the money be spent prior to then, additional sums could be appropriated or borrowed from unexpended resources in the emergency account or possibly even from regular development resources if the specific ACP countries should so agree. Responsibility for administration of this new provision lies with the Policy Planning and Coordination Section that is responsible for general development planning, not just for refugees. Hence, there should be considerable overall coordination between both refugee-related infrastructural assistance and the regular development programming process. Indeed, the assistance provided under article 204 will be incorporated into the regular implementation procedures used by the EC which are described in articles 215–224 of the Lomé Convention. The major difference is that the Article 204 aid can be spent on a more rapid basis.

EC delegates in African asylum countries will be responsible for initial program development, which further emphasizes the need for adequate host country coordination. Once general program areas are identified in collaboration with headquarters, the process of identifying specific projects will begin. EC officials estimate that by early 1986 some of the ICARA II projects may be ready for initial implementation. In the meantime the EC must begin to flesh out guidelines and policy regarding how the resources in Article 204 should be spent. For instance should it emphasize 5b or 5c activities? Should it emphasize projects in only a few major countries or try to spread the resources around to as many countries as possible? Should emphasis be given to refugee or returnee areas? Should the resources be spent quickly or meted out over the life of the agreement? Who should implement the projects? The EC directly? U.N. agencies? NGOs? What kinds of infrastructural projects should be supported? In general the EC has financed roadbuilding and similar activities, although there is a growing interest in programs that will enhance agricultural productivity and self-sufficiency – in other words, activities which will help to mitigate future emergency needs. Answers to many of the above questions will result from a process of mutual collaboration between the EC, the governments of EC members and host governments over the next few years.

The EC response to ICARA II, if somewhat unavoidably delayed, has been a very encouraging one. They have identified a focal point in the Commission for ICARA II follow-up, have developed a financial mechanism to fund refugee-related projects falling between traditional emergency and development aid categories, and have committed substantial additional funds to the endeavor. Now all that remains is for the EC to follow through with effective implementation. On this score, given the rather large sums of money that will be involved, additional EC personnel are likely to be needed to adequately monitor implementation. As it stands now only one person has part-time responsibility for the Article 204 provision. Even if substantial portions of the resources should be eventually channeled through UNDP, UNHCR other U.N. agencies or NGOs as opposed to direct EC implementation, there will be an expanded personnel requirement to monitor program activities.

On the whole, the EC has responded in a serious and considered way to the refugee-related development needs of Africa. Although all the details of the EC approach are as yet not known, it seems clear that it is headed in a direction entirely compatible with the themes of ICARA II. Indeed, EC officials admit that ICARA II had a direct bearing on the decision to include article 204 in the latest Lomé agreement.

Other Donors

Many of the donors discussed thus far have chosen to respond to ICARA II through bilateral channels. However, several others, especially those which lack a sufficient capacity to undertake independent development programming have chosen to contribute resources to the UNDP. Such was the case with Saudi Arabia, to name a key example. The availability of multilateral channels for ICARA II allows non-traditional donors to participate in African development programs. It also provides more flexibility to traditional donors who may not be in a position to study, design or implement projects in specific African countries because they lack posts in them, or because the posts are understaffed.

So far only a few donors and a modest amount of money have been channeled to the UNDP various financing mechanisms. Indeed, the $5 million Saudi Arabian pledge was disappointingly low to U.N. officials who had expected a figure closer to $30 or 40 million.[38] Over time, however, one can expect the UNDP to attract increments of resources for ICARA II projects from both major donors and non-traditional ones.

ADDITIONALITY REVISITED

Of all the concepts underpinning ICARA II, perhaps the most elusive is that of additionality.[39] As has been noted before, the concept itself can be defined easily. It refers simply to the notion that the resources a country of asylum receives for refugee-related development projects should not be provided at the expense of funds it would have otherwise received for its regular development program. In other words, refugee-hosting countries should receive new money for these special needs, so that regular development programming does not suffer. This is easy enough to understand. But operationalizing the concept is more difficult than defining it. In the final analysis, about the only way to know whether resources are additional is to determine if the legislature in a donor country has appropriated new funds for a certain activity. But even this test is not completely reliable. How does one determine whether the legislature might have increased regular development programs by a larger amount had new money for a new activity not been requested? In those cases where resources for development fluctuate in size or in programmatic emphasis, how does one determine when an appropriation is additional? Moreover, should one count money borrowed from other non-ICARA II African countries or non-African countries as additional? Certainly to the country receiving it, such aid is additional. In short, although seemingly a simple concept, additionality raises a number of definitional problems.

At its most elemental level additionality is favored by the Africans because – if adhered to by donors – it would provide them with more resources. On the other hand, many donors are uncomfortable with the idea, even if they agree with it in principle.

Notwithstanding the operational difficulties with this concept, as one examines the donor response to ICARA II for evidence of additionality one is driven to the conclusion that only very modest amounts of money can be considered truly additional. All of the donors present at ICARA II joined in the consensus on the Final Declaration and Programme of Action which stated that funds contributed for refugee-related development assistance should be additional. In keeping with the conditional nature of this phraseology, the donors approached the issue of additionality from a variety of perspectives. Some, like Japan, stated unequivocally that its contributions would not be additional. Others, like Italy and Norway, openly embraced the concept and pledged money which they claimed was additional. Still other donors, such as Finland, made pledges but did not indicate whether or not they represented additional resources (the presumption being that in most cases they were not). Finally, some donors have funded projects from both additional and existing resources. The United States Congress, for instance, has authorized the expenditure of up to $6.75 million in new money for ICARA II which was made available through March of 1986, while other projects have been funded from existing resources. Only the EC has made a significant commitment of additional resources.

Even where donors have emphasized that their contributions to ICARA II have been additional, closer scrutiny suggests that this is debatable. Take, for example, the case of Italy which pledged $15 million at ICARA II. Were these truly additional funds as claimed by Italy? The fact of the matter is that the Italian parliament voted a fixed amount of money for its foreign assistance budget in 1979 to last for five years. (In those five years, the assistance budget did gradually increase, but the overall five-year appropriation was fixed.) Since virtually all of this budget is spent in Africa, and since no additional sum was appropriated by the parliament for ICARA II, it seems fair to conclude that the money Italy pledged at ICARA II was not truly additional in character. In other words, these were resources that would have been spent elsewhere in the Italian development assistance program for Africa. As some Italian government officials have admitted, the primary purpose for claiming additionality was a political one, which had the desired effect: Africans greatly appreciated the Italian pledge and its support for the concept of additionality. Despite the apparent duplicity here, in all fairness, the Italian contribution to African relief and development programs has grown enormously in the last five years. In other words, almost everything Italy has done during that time can be seen as additional compared to its previous inactivity in development assistance. Viewed from this perspective, one can see how variable the perception of additionality can be.

Many donors find themselves in a difficult position insofar as securing truly additional resources are concerned. For instance, Canada, which had hoped to reach a foreign assistance level of 0.7 percent of its GNP by 1990, has experienced some budgetary retrenchment with the installation of a new conservative government in 1984. As a result, it will not reach level until 1995 or later. In the meantime less will be available than originally anticipated for development activities in general and for refugee-related development assistance in particular. Still, Canada's overall development budget is on the increase, if at a slower pace, and it is not unreasonable for it to fold its ICARA II projects into the regular development assistance budget pool. Unlike Italy, Canada has chosen to tell African governments squarely that any ICARA II projects it funds will have to be considered as part of the overall development effort. Funds for them will not be additional, in the sense that the Africans understand the term.

As humanitarian and emergency needs in Africa have increased donors are being asked to dig even deeper into their pockets to provide assistance. Longer range development efforts may have suffered to some extent as resources have been mobilized to address immediate needs. Donors do not question the need for either famine relief, refugee assistance or long-term development aid. But domestic pressures for resources and general economic conditions in many countries limit the availability of resources for foreign assistance. The resource pool is not inexhaustable. For these and other reasons donors have emphasized the need to establish program priorities in host countries. ICARA II projects must inevitably be considered on both their own merits and in relation to the merits of other development priorities. Most of the donors are prepared to work with the Africans to determine what these priorities should be.

Certainly, additionality should not be taken as the only litmus of success, although it is clearly one measure of success. Just as important is the quality of programs initiated under the rubric of ICARA II. New money is clearly not the only answer to meeting African development needs. Available development resources also must be spent more wisely. In this way, despite the leanness of assistance availabilities, their impact can be strengthened. Donor reluctance to rush large sums of additional resources into a relatively new form of assistance is not groundless. As the ICARA II process unfolds, however, one would hope that donors will be generous in meeting not only the more limited refugee-related development needs, but the general development predicament facing African countries as well. But in a period of widespread budgetary exigency, generosity may mean simply keeping pace with past assistance levels. In short, the question of ad-

ditionality must be understood and examined in the context of
budgetary realities.

As has been noted in several examples above, the financial and
organizational constraints facing donor reponse to ICARA II are
not insignificant. Neither are they unmanageable. On the organizational side, several donors, including the UK, FRG, Switzerland, the United States and several others, have developed administrative mechanisms and programs to finance refugee-related
development projects. In some cases these mechanisms have
operated quite smoothly while in others there have been bureaucratic tensions. Institutional jealousies, bureaucratic rivalries and
administrative obstacles can be overcome with a little persistence,
ingenuity and creativity. Donor coordination of their bilateral and
multilateral assistance programs and in some cases of their refugee and development ministries will be an essential ingredient of
successful response to ICARA II. The linkage of refugee aid and
development assistance has clear implications, then, not just in
the field, but for relationships between relevant donor country
ministries.

Overcoming the financial constraints is a more difficult task.
Donors face multiple requests for assistance, and must make
choices about what to fund and for how much. Refugee-related
development needs are weighed against other assistance requests,
and often do not surface as a major priority. This problem is
compounded when host governments lacking additional resources are unwilling to divert funds from regular development
programs. This presents a bit of a dilemma in cases where donors
truly are unable to expand their resource base. One way to
address this problem would be agreement between donors and
hosts whereby the donor would provide half of the amount necessary to finance a particular project from additional resources,
with the rest being garnered from the existing program. This
would limit the drawdown of ICARA II projects on the regular
development program, provide for new if smaller amounts of
additional resources, and thereby also limit the impact on already

strained donor country budgets. In some situations this kind of compromise might be an appropriate way to ensure that ICARA II projects are not completely ignored in favor of the regular development programs.

If donors had the will to do so, there are ways to finance refugee-related development projects with additional resources, if some creative thinking is brought to bear. In effect, however, the will to do this must exist at the highest political levels within donor country governments. It is insufficient that a ministry or agency here or there is committed to providing substantial additional resources. In the absence of a supportive executive, such commitments can quickly run afoul of the budgetary priorities of other ministries. In a very real sense, then, the financial success of endeavors like ICARA II depends on the sympathetic support of Heads of State or government. Unfortunately, ICARA II has been a low priority for many donor countries. Nor are the constituencies in support of refugee aid and development assistance so large or influential as to ensure that these activities reach a high place on the policy agenda. But neither have donor governments completely forgotten their responsibilities. Many of them persist in studying projects with a view toward eventual implementation. They may not provide levels of support commensurate with African expectations, but they are unlikely to ignore completely the commitments made and the principles articulated at ICARA II. Indeed, should donors follow through on all of the projects in which they have expressed serious interest, it would not be surprising to see nearly half of the ICARA II projects funded within five years. One could then debate from a quantitative standpoint whether the conference had been a success. However, in view of the many obstacles and constraints that have bedeviled ICARA II, there could be little doubt that this would be a major accomplishment, particularly if the process set in motion continues to respond to refugee-related development needs in the years to come.

NOTES

1. As of January 1986, only about a dozen ICARA projects had been initiated. However several other projects remain under consideration. About $54 million in resources were pledged toward 5c projects at ICARA II. But perhaps as much as two-thirds of this was from existing resources.
2. Belgium, for instance, expressed interest in a project in Burundi, but decided not to fund it after a closer review.
3. Finland and Italy, for instance, both wanted to fund the Dire Dawa food storage project in Ethiopia. The Italians were given the nod and the Finns financed a similar project in the Gambela region of Ethiopia. Similarly, the United States and Japan were both interested in the Kassala Water project in Sudan. The Japanese have begun field review of this project, leaving the United States to look elsewhere in Eastern Sudan for potential water project sites.
4. The Netherlands, for instance, expressed interest in about 15 projects, although clearly it had resources to fund only a few.
5. The United States, for instance, indicated its interest in reforestation and water projects not included in the documentation. Sweden, similarly, stressed that its ongoing development programming would continue to stress ICARA II-like projects, and the roughly $2 million it pledged at ICARA II has been spent on ongoing ICARA II-like projects in Angola, Zambia, Botswana and Mozambique.
6. See *Africa Research Bulletin,* 15 May 1981, p. 6011.
7. Much of the discussion in this section is based on the author's first-hand experience in the U.S. Department of State, where he worked on U.S. preparations for ICARA II.
8. See *United States Contributions to International Organizations: Report to the Congress for Fiscal Year 1983,* 32nd annual report, (Washington, D.C.: U.S. Department of State, 1983), pp. 19–20.
9. See the Report of the Secretary-General on the Results of ICARA, Table II, (June 1981).
10. U.S. intentions to 'participate fully' at ICARA II were announced by Secretary of State, George Shultz, at the World Affairs Council in Boston, on 15 February 1984, despite the desire of the Office of the Coordinator for Refugees to withhold such an announcement indefinitely. The announcement was made on the same day Shultz approved the decision to attend ICARA II. It is interesting to note that Secretary Shultz's speech in Boston was billed as a major statement on U.S. policy in Africa. However, in the question and answer period following the address, not a single question was asked about Africa. The audience apparently was more interested in the Central American issue. Sadly, this example illustrates how little attention Africa often commands in the United States. It is especially surprising that a World Affairs Council audience was so totally out of tune with the major purpose of the Secretary's address. This was perhaps an indication of the rough go ICARA II would have in attracting U.S. public attention.

11. RP recognized the need to begin studying projects which might be funded from existing resources shortly after ICARA II. In fact some $11 million of the available ARSFP resources would have lapsed back to the U.S. Treasury had they not been obligated prior to the end of fiscal year 1984. A scant two months would have been left after ICARA II to undertake studies and to obligate funds. Thus, it was essential to begin field review of the projects well before ICARA II, even if no pledge were to be made. The Office of the Coordinator for Refugees ineffectually objected that this review compromised the nonpledging stance.

12. State/RP draws its statutory authority from the Migration and Refugee Act of 1962 (Public Law 87–510, 76 Stat. 121) and the Refugee Act of 1980 (Public Law 96–212, 94 Stat. 109). AID was created in 1961 under revisions to the Foreign Assistance Act. See, Executive Order 10973, Section 102 and the Foreign Assistance Act, 26/FR 10608 Sections 1–3, in *Legislation on Foreign Relations Through 1978,* U.S. Congress, February 1979, Vol I, pp. 228–239.

13. Since ICARA II the U.S. government has funded four projects from its ARSFP account. Only one of these, the Shaba roads project in Zaire ($3.6 million), was included in the ICARA documentation. The other projects included reforestation in Rwanda ($2.5 million), and increases in funding to a project in Chad ($.5 million) and the Gedaref water project in Sudan ($5.5 million). An Aquaculture project in Zambia has been funded through RP's special projects budget, and AID has obligated $2.5 million for a health project, and $2.25 million for a water project, both in the Shaba region of Zaire. A total of $10.77 million in the ARSFP account is being reserved for a rehabilitation project in Uganda and refugee settlement projects in Somalia.

14. For a draft of this bill and comments by Representative Weiss, see; *Congressional Record,* 98th Cong., 2nd sess., 1984, Vol. 130, no. 109, pp. E 3720–3722.

15. See House Resolution 1239 in *Congressional Record,* 99th Cong. 1st sess., 1985, Vol. 131, no. 1-Part II, pp. E 99–100.

16. See the full House Appropriations Committee Report accompanying H.R. 1239, p. 7. The report suggested that the $12.5 million might also be used for expediting the migration of Ethiopia's Falashas and their relocation in Israel.

17. *Ibid.,* pp. 2 and 6.

18. For a text of the African Famine Relief and Recovery Act of 1985 see Public Law 99–8, 99 Stat. 21, April 2, 1985; and Public Law 99–10, 99 Stat. 27, April 4, 1985.

19. See HR 1239, for language on provision of refugee assistance.

20. See the text of the U.S. address to ICARA II, which was delivered by U.S. Attorney-General, William French Smith, who headed the U.S. delegation.

21. This is based on comments made by U.K. officials interviewed in Geneva and London (November 1984 and June 1985). The British Refugee Council had recommended that the UK make available 25 million pounds for ICARA II. See 'Africa's Refugee Crisis: New Directions for Assistance, Aid and Development' (British Refugee Council, June 1984). p. 11. The government's response fell 20 million pounds short of this proposal illustrating that

the problem of availability of additional resources is not limited to the United States alone. In fact, BRC officials believe that the UK government's response was reasonably good given the budgetary constraints under which it operated.

22. See *Terms of Reference: ICARA II Refugee-Related Infrastructure Projects.* (London: Overseas Development Administration, 1984).

23. ICARA II was debated under UNGA agenda item 90. See the Third Committee resolution, A/39/C3/L.43.

24. See the FRG Statement to ICARA II, delivered by Minister of State, Alois Mertes. Geneva: 9–11 July 1984.

25. *Ibid.*

26. Based on discussions with FRG officials in Geneva and Bonn (November 1984 and May 1985).

27. Information in this section was obtained primarily through the author's interviews with Italian officials in Rome, Geneva and Washington, D.C. (November 1984, March and May 1985).

28. Interview with Japanese officials in Geneva (November 1984).

29. *Ibid.*

30. See A/39/402/Add. 1, p. 22.

31. For details on Nordic country response to ICARA II see; A/39/402/Add. 1. On the Swedish situation, the observations made above are based on interviews with Swedish government officials (June 1985).

32. For a description of this project see; *Mechanization of Agriculture in the Refugee Settlement Areas of The Eastern Sudan: A Summary of the Joint Finnish-Sudanese Project Review Mission* (Helsinki: Finnida, December 1984). Much of the information in the section on Finland was obtained through interviews with Finnish government officials in Helsinki (May 1985).

33. See Finland's statement at ICARA II, delivered by Mr. Martti Ahtisaari, Undersecretary of State, Ministry of Foreign Affairs, 10 July 1984.

34. Based on interviews with Finnida and Political Department officials in Helsinki (May 1985).

35. Much of the information presented in this section was obtained through interviews with EC officials in Brussels (May 1985).

36. See the so-called Dury Report; *The Draft Report on Assistance to Refugees in Developing Countries,* compiled by the Committee on Development and Cooperation for the European Parliament, 1983.

37. For a complete text of the Third ACP-EC Convention signed at Lomé on 8 December 1984, see; *The Courier* No. 89 (January-February 1985). Article 204 can be found at p. 47.

38. U.N. officials had counted on a substantial commitment of resources from the Gulf states to give ICARA II some initial momentum. The reason for the lower than expected response is not entirely clear, although it was rumored that Saudi Arabia was dissatisfied over the selection of the President of the conference.

39. For a lucid discussion on the subject of additionality see Martin Barber, 'Voluntary Agency Perspectives on Refugee Aid and Development', paper presented at the ICVA General Conference, Dakar, Senegal, (May 1985).

CHAPTER 5

Host Country Response to ICARA II

Uige, Dukwe, Cankuzo, Hararghe, Gedo, Kibungo, Kassala, Mwinilunga, Ituri: most people have never heard of these places. They do not evoke images of importance like centers of power and international decision making do. But in the end, the success or failure of ICARA II will depend as much upon what happens in these places as in New York, or Geneva, or in the major capitals of the Western World. The burdens which ICARA II presumes to address are found in these and other hinterland areas of a continent which itself – however strongly we resist the conclusion – has been viewed by many as hinterland in the affairs of international power politics. The majority of African refugees reside in remote and poorly developed regions like those mentioned above. These are the front lines in the battle to address refugee-related development burdens.

Khartoum, Mogadishu, Kigali, Lusaka, Addis Ababa and Kampala – to give but a few examples – may strike a more familiar note with the reader. The success of ICARA II hinges on decisions made in these places too. The African capitals are not on the front lines: most African refugees reside in the rural areas and in many cases far away from the seats of national government. But what happens in the capital cities is also important. The battle on the front lines will be mounted and directed from the capitals. They will be the focal point for coordination of U.N. donor country, and NGO activity. The host government, working with the donor community will have much to do with how well refugee aid and development assistance can be integrated.

This chapter focuses on the problems host countries will face in responding to ICARA II, whether on the front lines or in the capitals. To understand these problems we will begin with a discussion of the burden concept which underlies the whole ICARA II enterprise. This will be followed by a specific examination of the problems which are being encountered in host countries as implementation of ICARA II projects proceeds. Then several models of host country coordination of refugee and development assistance will be examined.

THE CONCEPT OF THE BURDEN

The primary justification for ICARA II and a central theme of those who advocate the linkage of refugee and development assistance is that refugees impose burdens on the development capacity, the economic infrastructure and the social systems of receiving countries. As noted in chapter two, there is widespread agreement that refugees create special burdens on host countries even though absolute quantitative verification of the burden is not possible. But it is not clear that everyone has the same perception of the nature of the burden. It will be useful, then, to examine this concept more closely, so that we clearly understand what it is, how it is perceived and how it can vary from one context to another.

Twin Perspectives

We must begin with the question: who or what is it that is burdened by refugees? There are two answers to this question: 1. the economic and social infrastructure of the host country, and; 2. the people of the host country, especially those living in the most heavily refugee-affected areas. These two aspects are obviously related, but may not always be subject to the same remedy. ICARA II emphasizes the first aspect of the burden; that is helping the host government cope with the burden on its economic infrastructure. This can be seen by breaking down the ICARA II projects into sectors. About $111 million of ICARA II projects are for roads, bridges, port facilities and energy infrastructure. About $49 million is for water supply infrastructure and equipment. Of the projects devoted to education and training, nearly $74 million worth of the entire $90 million package is for construction of school buildings. Similarly, about $46 million of the $65 million devoted to health is for construction of hospitals (and in some cases clinics), and $6.5 million of the $8.7 million devoted to social systems is for construction of buildings. The ICARA II request for agriculture, forestry and fisheries projects amounted to roughly $105 million. Of this, some $20 million is for heavy equipment and machinery and $20 million for reforestation. In short, the projects submitted to ICARA II are biased heavily toward physical infrastructure, and are very short on the human dimension of the development burden. Roughly 80 percent of the total value of ICARA II projects is for infrastructure.[1]

This in itself is not a problem, for few would deny the need for the kind of infrastructural inputs anticipated in these projects. The problem is that development is as much a function of strengthening community organization, as well as the management capacities and technical expertise of people in a developing country. A school without good teachers or adequate educational materials will not advance the education of refugees or host country nationals. A hospital in a district center will not answer the most immediate primary health care needs of refugees and the rural host country population. Nor will clinics without trained personnel and medical supplies improve the primary health care needs of people in the hinterlands. Building roads, bridges and other physical infrastructure is necessary to interlink an economy, but may have only a remote impact on refugees and local people unless employment and marketing opportunities are created for them in the process. Infrastructure itself has only a long-term payoff for the average individual. However, if implemented using local materials, local labor and initiative, more immediate positive outcomes for rural host and refugee programs are possible.

In other words, the way in which the primarily infrastructural projects are implemented will determine whether they address both elements of the burden or only the infrastructure needs themselves. If local needs are taken into account then the impact of the projects on both the infrastructure and on the burden borne by the population will be positive. It is not essential that all of the ICARA II projects address the specific needs of refugees and the host population. But to the extent that the African governments have claimed a need for additional resources to reduce the infrastructural burden and to benefit both refugees and host country nationals, it would be appropriate for projects to take the needs of the latter into explicit account.

African Views on the Burden

For many African governments, ICARA II represented a way to secure much needed resources for infrastructural development in refugee-affected regions of their countries. They argued, quite justifiably, that the brunt of the refugee burden had been borne by them. They pointed out that, unlike the Asian refugee situation, their generosity in according asylum to refugees made resettlement programs to Western countries largely unnecessary. On the other hand, their generous asylum policies have resulted in much higher costs and strains on their economies. Hence, they support the concept of international burden sharing. Donors should be prepared to assist host countries, the Africans argued, to cope with the burdens. Moreover, this assistance should be additional to regular development needs. In preparing their submissions for ICARA II, African governments put most of their emphasis on the infrastructural element of the burden. To be sure, most of the projects are in refugee-impacted areas, and hence should benefit to some extent both refugees and the local population. But the projects were devised primarily by government officials, often without adequate consultation with local groups or refugees. Many of them reflect a greater concern for physical infrastructure rather than for strengthening the local organizational capacities or for addressing other more immediate development needs at the local level.

The Variable Nature of the Burden

A subject that merits closer scrutiny concerns the variable nature of the refugee burden. One should not assume that just because a country hosts refugees, that it automatically shoulders an immense burden. Indeed, the gravity of the burden varies between and even within countries, based on a number of factors, including the size of the refugee population, the ratio of refugees to the host country or regional population, the fragility of the refugee-impacted area's environment, the length of time refugees have been present, the availability of arable land, the cultural and ethnic make-up of the refugee and host country population (which can have security implications), and the policies of the host government toward the refugees. Several examples will serve to illustrate how the burdens vary from one context to another.

At the time of ICARA II, Sudan had a refugee population of about 665,000, including roughly 200,000 Ugandans in the south and 465,000 Ethiopians in the East. Most of the Ethiopians were spontaneously settled in the urban areas or on rural wage settlements, but about 160,000 remained in camps. In the east, refugees have flooded the job market, strained government capacities to provide social services, and placed additional pressure on already scarce water supplies. The burden is a clear and obvious one. Still, even here, refugees – especially the spontaneously settled ones – also produce and consume, and hence contribute to the economic life of the area.[2] In the south of Sudan, the refugee situation is somewhat different. In this area, where arable land is more plentiful, many refugees have spontaneously settled, and in many cases have attained agricultural self-sufficiency. They pose less of a burden on the local economy than do refugees in the east. Still, there are added pressures for health and educational services, which the government is not in a position to provide without assistance. (Recently, the security situation in the south has deteriorated to such an extent that most development activities there have been suspended.) In Sudan, then, the seriousness and nature of the refugee burden varies from region to region. On the whole, however, it is clear that major burdens do exist. These have been heightened even more dramatically as the drought has hit millions of Sudanese nationals and provoked an influx of 450,000 additional drought victims and refugees from Chad and Ethiopia. Under these circumstances, no one should doubt the grave pressures placed by refugees on Sudan's economic and social infrastructure.

Another country where refugees have created fairly significant burdens is Somalia. Although precise figures on the number of refugees there have been difficult to determine, there is little doubt that several hundred thousand were spontaneously assimilated in addition to the 500,000–700,000 who reside in official refugee camps. The ratio of refugees to the host population is the highest in Africa; about 3 or 4 : 1. This has placed a significant strain on the Somali government's capacity to provide health services to its own and the refugee population. On the other hand, the creation of the Refugee Health Unit (RHU) has strengthened the capacity of Somalia's Ministry of Health to provide primary health care not only to refugees but rural Somalis as well. Over the long run the host population should benefit from the refugee presence in terms of improved rural health care. Additional pressure has been placed on rangelands in Somalia by the livestock of spontaneously settled refugees. Deforestation has been aggravated by camp refugees. Moreover, possibilities for self-reliant agricultural activities in refugee camp areas have been severely limited by the lack of arable land and water resources, and the unwillingness of the government, until a few years ago, to consider a policy of local settlement and integration for refugees.

Although they are hardly the only countries that have demonstrable refugee-related development burdens. Sudan and Somalia (which together account for about half of Africa's refugees) are good cases where refugees on the whole have strained rather than benefitted the host country economy. However, in some countries or at least in parts of them, refugees have been a net plus. For instance, in Tanzania, where most of the refugee population of about 170,000 has been present for a decade or more, refugees have become productive contributors to the national economy. Most of them live in settlements which have been handed over to government administration. Many of these villages were developed in virgin lands, and thus represent a net increase in cultivated acreage for Tanzania. Nevertheless, some settlements have been much more successful than others. Refugees in Katumba constitute about 35–40 percent of the population but produce 90 percent of the area's crops. Nearby at Mwesi, the National Milling Company buys surpluses from refugee cooperatives. Refugees at Mwesi are cultivating previously virgin lands. They even pay taxes to the Tanzanian government. Improvements in infrastructure could further strengthen the self-reliance of the refugees and in some cases hasten their integration into the regional and national economies. But in this case the projects are not necessary as an answer to a serious burden. Rather they represent a sensible next step in Tanzania's refugee settlement policy.

The Tanzanian situation differs from that prevailing in most of Somalia and in Eastern Sudan. Good land and water is readily available, and the refugees are agriculturalists. With these three primary ingredients – land, water and labor – coupled with initial external inputs of seeds and implements, refugees can achieve self-reliance and even contribute to economic development in the host country.[3] Tanzania's progressive policy toward refugees has further contributed to this end. In short, refugees have been less a burden than a benefit in Tanzania.

Similarly, in Haut Zaire refugees from Uganda have settled on virgin lands, have become virtually self-reliant in food production, and created a whole new economy in the area. International resources have been invested in the improvement of hospital and health infrastructure, which had fallen into disuse or disrepair prior to the refugee influx. In other parts of Zaire, such as Shaba and the Kinshasa region, the presence of refugees has not had so salubrious an impact. But in Haut Zaire, as in most of Tanzania, refugees have stimulated rather than detracted from development.

Another example illustrates how within a country refugees can in one region pose substantial burdens but in another have beneficial effects. On the surface, Rwanda would appear to have one of the most severe refugee burdens on the continent of Africa. Indeed, its per capita GNP of $250 is one of the lowest and its population growth rate of 3.7 percent one of the highest in the world. As a land-locked country with a population density of over 300 persons per square mile,[4] its capacity to absorb the 54,000 refugees who have sought asylum there is limited. The recent influx of 36,000 persons from Uganda has underscored Rwandan sensitivities to pressures on the land, especially in respect to the semi-pastoralist Banyarwandans who require more land than do agriculturalists.

Still some refugees have contributed to Rwanda's economy and impose less of a burden. For instance, Burundian refugees have been settled in Rukomo since 1972. There are now 8,000 refugees living there. The land they originally were settled on was previously abandoned by Tutsis. The refugees energetically developed the area. Their success in this endeavor caused many native Rwandan's to gravitate into the Rukomo sector which has since become the commercial center of the Mutara region. The Burundian refugees have stimulated trading in the area. Ironically, the population pressures and other infrastructural kinds of burdens that exist in and around Rukomo, might be attributed to the influx or Rwandans rather than the Burundi refugees themselves.[5] Still, as the population of the whole area grows, including that of the refugees, demands for education and health services will increase, and pressures on the land will grow. In this sence certain burdens are generated by the refugees and Rwandans in the area, and the Rwandan ICARA II proposals focus primarily on the need for schools and health clinics there.

The recent influx of people from Uganda presents a more straightforward situation where refugees are a strain on rather than a benefit to the local economy in Rwanda. In areas such as Byumba and Kibungo Prefectures, the need for land and pasture development to accommodate both refugees and the host populations is significant. Land, which is the most precious resource in Rwanda, must be husbanded ever more carefully as the population pressure from refugees and Rwandans increases.

The character of the refugee burden on each of the African countries which submitted ICARA II proposals must ultimately be assessed on a case-by-case basis. It is not within the scope of this study to conduct such an analysis, but the cases cited above help to illustrate the variability of the refugee burden. For those who are interested in a country-by-country assessment of the impact of refugees the ICARA II documentation is as thorough a source as any.[6] It is worth observing, however, that some of the countries which submitted proposals have such relatively small refugee populations that they have failed to excite a great deal of donor interest. These countries include: Botswana (5,000 refugees), Cameroon (4,000), Chad (7,000), Kenya (6,000) and Swaziland (7,000). The infrastructural needs of the countries with smaller refugee (or returnee) populations seem to pale by comparison to other countries which have been inundated with refugees. But this should not lead one to conclude that legitimate needs do not exist which could be addressed by infrastructural assistance. Indeed, most of these countries submitted modest requests befitting the more modest nature of the burdens they face.

The African host countries in many cases have had to cope with several major and interrelated problems in implementing ICARA II projects and in their efforts to link development and refugee planning more closely. These problems include: how to increase coordination between their refugee and development ministries, how to cope with limited absorptive capacity and to meet recurrent costs of infrastructural projects, how to successfully coordinate with donors and the U.N. system, and how to cope with the drought, and in some cases, continuing political instability.

Inter-Ministerial Coordination of Development and Refugee Aid

African asylum countries have devised a wide variety of organizational strategies for dealing with refugees on one hand and with development planning on the other. (Only in a few cases, however, is there a direct link between agencies responsible for refugees and development-related ministries.) Indeed, each country's approach to refugee and development planning is unique. Nevertheless, in reference to the refugee element three general approaches have been adopted by most of the countries. First, in the countries with the largest refugee/returnee problems, largely autonomous refugee commissions have been established. In Somalia there is the National Refugee Commission (NRC), in Ethiopia the Relief and Rehabilitation Commission (RRC), and in Sudan the Office of the Commissioner for Refugees (COR). Second, in most other countries, responsibility for refugees has been placed within an existing ministry. In some cases these ministries have development-related responsibilities. Examples include Uganda's Ministry of Culture and Community Development and Angola's Office of the Secretary of State for Social

Affairs. In Botswana the Office of the President is responsible for refugees. In other cases the responsible refugee agency has little or no connection with the development-related ministries. In Zambia, for instance, the Office of the Refugee Commissioner is housed in the defense and security division of the Ministry of Home Affairs. In Zaire, the Foreign Ministry handles all refugee matters including monitoring of the ICARA II infrastructural projects. Most development ministries in Zaire are only secondarily involved in oversight of ICARA projects, although in the case of the U.S.-funded roads project in Shaba, the Ministry of Roads is the primary implementor. Third, in a relatively few countries, efforts have been made to integrate refugee planning more explicitly into the overall development planning process. In Burundi, for example, refugee matters are handled by the Ministry of the Interior. However, the Minister of Planning in the President's Office establishes general development priorities and selects specific projects, including refugee-related ones. In addition, an interministerial committee was established to coordinate the refugee and development aspects of preparations for ICARA II. Similarly, in Lesotho, the Ministry for Interior handles refugee affairs subject to oversight of an interministerial committee.

The need for coordination of refugee and development planning is addressed best in the third set of examples cited above. In the first and second set of examples coordination often has been wanting. For example, in Somalia, the NRC has duplicated many responsibilities in monitoring refugee situations that already exist in the line ministries for development. Somalia's ICARA II projects reflected the priorities established by NRC but the Ministry of Planning has expressed doubts that they are consistent with its own priorities for development programming in the country as a whole. From the Ministry of Planning's perspective many of the highly rated ICARA II projects may in fact be very low priorities when stacked up against other development needs.[7] It is not clear that the NRC, Planning and other main-line development ministries communicated as closely as would have been desirable. Nor is it clear that they agree on how to determine the validity and priority of refugee-related development projects. Perhaps as Somalia's steering committee for local settlement of refugees

120

matures (the structure and role of this entity are described below), greater collaboration between the NRC and Ministry of Planning will be manifested.

The problem of coordination is not limited to cases where autonomous refugee commissions have been established. Even where the refugee fuction is housed within a particular development agency, the need for interministerial consultation and collaboration on the design and implementation of ICARA II projects is necessary. Rarely do the offices responsible for refugees have a sufficient number of personnel trained in the various fields of development expertise. Hence, they are not in a position to adequately oversee the design and implementation of infrastructural projects. Their role should be rather more like that which the UNHCR has adopted in respect to the U.N. development agencies. In other words, they should play a catalytic role by seeking to draw the attention of development ministries to refugee-related development projects. As a general rule, having secured the interest of relevant development agencies, the refugee agency should be ready to step back and allow the former – assuming that they are willing and able to do so – to oversee day-to-day implementation. The problem with a direct refugee agency implementing role is that it calls for the establishment of duplicative bureaucratic functions, which is unnecessary at a minimum, and potentially counterproductive.

A major need within African governments is for increased communication between refugee and development ministries, and development of a more explicit strategy for handling refugee-related development projects – one which would define explicitly the authorities and responsibilities of respective agencies. Unless governments carefully think through these relationships the successful implementation of ICARA II projects will be hampered.

Absorptive Capacity/Recurrent Cost Issues

The ability of the host countries to absorb assistance effectively and to meet the running costs of development projects, has been a source of concern and debate in the context of ICARA II. Donors raised these issues as potential problems prior to ICARA II and the technical team tried to assay their relevance on a project-by-project basis. The issues continue to be relevant as discussions on project implementation proceed. A complicating factor regarding the absorptive capacity question is the drought, which has stretched the manpower resources of many refugee hosting countries beyond the limit. Broken down to its most elemental level, the absorptive capacity problem rests on whether the host government has enough and the right kind of personnel. If the level of assistance provided to a country overloads its capacity to implement projects, its effectiveness will diminish and the quality of projects will suffer.

There are ways to overcome these problems on an individual project basis. The most obvious is for the project to provide for additional technical personnel to assist the host government where it is lacking. Some, but not all, of the ICARA II projects take this factor into explicit account. But there is another aspect to the absorptive capacity problem which is less easily addressed. It concerns the actual feasibility study stage. African countries have faced multiple requests from donor countries to receive not only technical missions for ICARA II projects, but others assessing the immediate emergency needs. In some cases, these requests have been so numerous that the host countries have been unable to prepare adequately for them. Donors must take this into account, and not simply use it as an excuse to defer or cancel funding for ICARA II projects. The reality simply is that many of the countries engulfed by drought are often not in a position to divert precious manpower resources into preparing for ICARA II technical missions. Indeed, donors should pay especially close attention to how they might strengthen the managerial capacity of relevant host country ministries by lending them needed personnel. Over the long run, this kind of management infrastructure may turn out to be more critical than the physical infrastructure proposed by ICARA II.

The recurrent cost issue also requires careful attention as donors and hosts begin to discuss implementation of specific projects. Because of the infrastructural nature of the majority of the ICARA II projects, the recurrent cost issue is even more critical. Schools, hospitals, and clinics can be built but if they lack adequate staff or material inputs to function as intended, then resources will have been spent unwisely. Maintenance of roads and buildings must be considered also. As donors and host countries think through the implications of recurrent costs, they may find the price tag of the projects increasing substantially. In some cases donors may be willing to carry the recurrent costs as part of the financing of the project, but in others, the host country may be expected to do so. In any case, recurrent costs must be explicitly dealt with as projects are initiated.

Coordination with Donors and the United Nations System

It should be clear from the foregoing that the host countries need to coordinate not only their own inter-agency activities, but their relations with the donors and the U.N. agencies as well. In short, the success of the endeavor will rest to a very large extent on how well the various strands of external support eventually converge in the host country itself. Several steps can be taken (and to a certain extent are being taken), to give this process some coherence. First, the host countries must insist that ICARA II projects be given priority consideration. If the host governments lose enthusiasm, it is likely that donor interest will diminish as well. Second, the host governments should continue to work closely with the UNDP resident representatives to ensure that ICARA II projects are promoted among donor field representatives. Third, the donor country roundtables and CGs should be encouraged to consider ICARA II projects as part of discussions on overall development planning. In the absence of these steps, ICARA II follow-up in the host countries will be inevitably more haphazard and less effective.

Impact of the Drought

If the African drought has kept donor countries, the U.N. system and NGOs scrambling, it has overwhelmed many of the African governments. Indeed, the drought has had a generally enervating effect on the institutional capacity of the entire international community to respond to ICARA II. But the impact has been felt most keenly in the drought-stricken countries themselves. Twelve of the nineteen African governments which submitted projects were on the list of seriously drought affected countries in 1985.

These included: Angola, Botswana, Burundi, Chad, Ethiopia, Kenya, Lesotho, Rwanda, Somalia, Sudan, Tanzania, and Zambia. Of these the most seriously affected have been Ethiopia, Sudan and Chad.[8] For many of these governments the chief impact of drought on ICARA II follow-up has been to siphon attention and already meager manpower and material resources away from it to meet emergency needs. As a consequence, many have not been adequately prepared to receive ICARA II technical missions from donors, which in some cases have been postponed.[9]

Despite the generally depressing affect that the drought has had on the ability to marshall funds for development, there may be positive longer term spin-offs. Both the UNOEOA and the various drought coordination mechanisms established in key drought-affected countries profess a concern about the need to move quickly toward rehabilitation and drought prevention. If these new organizational mechanisms are able to follow through on their stated intentions as the emergency abates, then a vigorous approach to tackling longer term development issues, including those addressed by ICARA II, may ensue.

MODELS OF REFUGEE/DEVELOPMENT COORDINATION

There is probably no single best approach to coordinating refugee and development assistance. The refugee and development circumstances of each asylum country vary, as do their administrative practices, organizational strengths and weaknesses. Nevertheless, there are basic steps that can be taken by governments in cooperation with U.N. agencies and donors to facilitate coordination. The cases analyzed below are not exhaustive but do illustrate the kinds of steps that can be taken to promote linkages between refugee and development assistance.

Somalia

With one of the two largest refugee populations in Africa, Somalia has borne substantial additional domestic burdens. Hundreds of thousands of refugees have been housed in camps where they have received international assistance. Tens of thousands more have spontaneously assimilated and have received no formal assistance.

In March 1983, the government of Somalia announced its intention to encourage local settlement of refugees who did not wish to repatriate to Ethiopia. Many of the refugees had resided in camps for as long as four years, and the government did not believe that conditions in Ethiopia would support repatriation (a belief that has been challenged since with the spontaneous repatriation of large numbers of refugees). Thus, it chose to emphasize the local settlement option as a more appropriate durable solution.

Local settlement of refugees bridges the gap between refugee and development assistance. Indeed, the development implications of settlement of refugees are critical, especially over the long run. While the UNHCR takes primary responsibility for refugee settlements in the short run (usually about four years), the host country must be prepared eventually to take over responsibility for them. Especially where refugees are to be integrated with the host population, the development implications are important from the very outset of settlement activities. Even pure refugee settlements must from the beginning anticipate longer term development issues including where they are sited, how land and water development will proceed, and whether refugee produce will have access to markets. In other words, refugee settlement programs require coordination of refugee and development assistance.

In Somalia, administrative structures have been created to bring together relevant development and refugee organizations to oversee implementation of the settlement policy. The structure consists of a Steering Committee, Technical Unit and executing agencies. The Steering Committee is chaired by the NRC and includes representatives of the government's Ministry of Planning, the UNDP and UNHCR. In other words, the lead refugee and development agencies within the government and the U.N. system have input into the settlement process. A Technical Unit, which is composed of specialists in rural settlement, agronomy, water development and physical planning, is responsible for reviewing the technical feasibility of projects submitted by potential executing agencies, including NGOs. Although the settlement policy has gotten off to a slow start, the machinery to implement it is at least in place.[10]

It is beyond the scope of this study to examine all of the details surrounding implementation of Somalia's settlement policy.[11] For our purposes it is enough to emphasize the role of the Steering Committee as a vehicle for coordinating refugee and development inputs. Although in this case the Committee and its Technical Unit have been established explicitly to oversee the settlement policy, it is an organizational model of how ICARA II projects could be handled in the future. Each asylum country could establish a steering group to coordinate ICARA II follow-up among relevant host country ministries, the UNDP, UNHCR, and donor governments. New projects could be identified and reviewed and their implementation monitored locally. Nor need steering committees be formal institutions. Informal consultations of this sort could be equally useful.

The lesson from the Somali case is that cooperative arrangements between the U.N. system and host country ministries can facilitate the linkage of refugee aid and development assistance. Moreover, local settlement efforts are not that far removed in kind from the infrastructural projects entertained by ICARA II. Each can be implemented through similar organizational arrangements.

Sudan

Nowhere has the burden of refugees in Africa been more apparent than in Sudan. Indeed, in the year following ICARA II, an additional 400,000 refugees and drought victims fled into Sudan from Chad and Ethiopia, swelling the number of refugees to over a million. The lack of adequate infrastructure in the drought and refugee-affected areas was made painfully obvious during the latest influx of population from neighboring states. Poor roads, inadequate storage facilities and insufficient water infrastructure hampered the emergency relief efforts. The need for such infrastructure both as a means for development and for mitigation of the emergency situation was etched in stark relief.[12]

Because of the great needs in Sudan, it is all the more important that relief and development assistance be marshalled effectively.

ICARA II assistance is no exception. Sudan submitted thirty infrastructural projects at ICARA II which totalled over $90 million. This represents a substantial potential investment and therefore should be carefully studied and implemented to ensure compatibility with existing development priorities. Indeed, of the thirty projects submitted, nearly two-thirds have attracted expressions of donor country interest, although only a few were actually under implementation by the summer of 1985.[13]

Like many of the other African asylum countries, Sudan has experienced severe drought since ICARA II. Donors have been slow to respond to longer-term infrastructural assistance since drought response has occupied most of their attention and energy. Indeed, the COR which is responsible for monitoring ICARA II follow-up in Sudan, has been preoccupied with the emergency, as have been many of the pertinent U.N. agencies, including the UNHCR and UNDP.

At least initially, there was an effort in Sudan to coordinate the ICARA II follow-up activities. In the fall of 1984, the UNDP held meetings with the donor countries and the UNHCR in an effort to establish some rudimentary in-country coordination and communication regarding implementation of ICARA II projects. These efforts were largely suspended, however, when the emergency hit full force. Since then ICARA II follow-up has been overshadowed by immediate needs. Although the UNDP in cooperation with COR continues to monitor ICARA II follow-up, there has been little time to engage in active promotion or to convene regular ICARA II follow-up meetings for all relevant actors in Sudan. As soon as circumstances permit, these activities should be resumed by the UNDP.

Another manifestation of coordination occurred in southern Sudan where the UNDP and UNHCR conducted joint reviews of refugee and development needs and where collaboration in project design and implementation was initiated in the spring of 1984. Unfortunately, these initial efforts have been overtaken by political instability in the south and the degree of UNHCR/UNDP collaboration evidenced there has yet to be matched anywhere else in Sudan.

Nevertheless, the example has been set, and could, when circumstances permit, be reinstituted and expanded. Coupled with this is the need for the COR to closely collaborate with the major development ministries at both the national and regional levels. Some interministerial collaboration did occur during the preparation of Sudan's ICARA II submission, but it is more difficult to ensure that adequate collaboration persists into the actual implementation phase. Similarly, it was one thing for the COR and development ministries to collaborate on preparation of the ICARA II documentation, for which there were a defined deadline, guidelines and a scope of work, and quite another to institutionalize such collaboration in an ongoing way. In Sudan, as in the other ICARA II countries, it is the latter which must be achieved if ICARA II is to have anything but a fleeting impact. Indeed, the emphasis many have placed on ICARA II as being a long-term process is perhaps most fitting in this context. This is so ultimately because the success of ICARA II and the effort to link refugee and development activities, will rest on the ability of relevant host government ministries to implement projects and to coordinate future refugee and development programming. In many of the key ICARA II countries, including Sudan, the process of interministerial coordination between refugee and development assistance has only just begun. It is a process that ICARA II initiated, that individual ministries should continue to grapple with, and that U.N. agenices and donors should do their best to stimulate and encourage.

Adapting Existing Models

As has been mentioned in several previous connections, the countries which submitted proposals to ICARA II, already have mechanisms for coordination of their development programming with U.N. agenices and donor countries. Kenya, Somalia, Sudan, Uganda, Zaire, and Zambia, for instance, maintain ongoing Consultative Group meetings led by the World Bank. Other less formal but often rigorous consultations are coordinated by the UNDP through round table discussions and are conducted in most developing countries. In general the ICARA II submissions were not subjected to these development review processes. Nor have these consultation processes normally encompassed refugee or emergency assistance. But clearly infrastructural projects in refugee-impacted areas have substantial development implications, and this relatively new form of assistance should be subject to the review of these consultative mechanisms to ensure complementarity with regular development programming.

However, host countries may be reluctant to accept full integration of ICARA II projects into these development programming fora in the absence of assurances of additional funding. Competition between mainstream development ministries for available development resources is already keen. The inclusion of refugee-related projects would only exacerbate this, and it is unlikely that too many host countries will attach a high priority to them unless additional resources are forthcoming.

Thus, adapting existing models to ensure coordination of refugee-related and regular development assistance may not be easy. It will require some accommodation between donor and host countries which would link the notions of additionality and complementarity. As discussed in the previous chapter this might take the form of an agreement by donors to finance with additional resources half of any ICARA II projects consistent with the country development strategy, provided the host country is willing to fund the other half with resources from the regular program. Other kinds of tradeoffs are also conceivable. The point is that donors are unlikely to achieve the goal of complementarity without providing some additional funds and host countries are unlikely to receive additional funds unless they take steps to ensure the harmonization of the refugee-related and regular development programs. In the Final Declaration and Programme of Action of ICARA II, the donor and host countries seemed to strike an initial bargain calling for both additionality and complementarity. But putting the rhetoric into action remains an uncompleted challenge.

REFUGEE AND HOST NATIONAL PARTICIPATION

Of the 130 million people who reside in the original 14 countries which submitted proposals to ICARA II, as much as a quarter to a third, or about 35–40 million live in refugee-affected areas. But so far, neither their voices, nor those of the refugees, have been solicited actively by planners and implementors of ICARA II. Instead ICARA II has been to a large extent a product of the interaction between governments, international agencies and, to some extent, NGOs. Refugees and host country nationals in refugee-affected areas have not been centrally engaged in project identification or implementation. They have been treated as beneficiaries, but rarely have they been an integral part of the decision-making process. This explains in part why ICARA II emphasized the infrastructural element of the refugee burden, rather than the more immediate needs of the host population or the refugees.

In theory, at least, it would be desirable to develop ways in which the local population and refugees could be included in the decision-making loop. NGOs and the U.N. agencies, themselves, have at least rhetorically supported this concept.[14] But it is not so easy to make it work in practice, even where governments and agencies are supportive. At a very basic level, traditional institutions for articulation of host population and refugee views may be nonexistent, poorly developed, or biased toward the views of a minority. On the other hand, one could call into question the right of external entities to dictate to people at the grass roots how they must be organized to be eligible for fuller participation in decision making about programs intended to meet their needs. But these considerations should not prevent governments, IOs and NGOs at a minimum from seeking out and listening to the voices of those who are likely to be affected most by refugee-related development aid.[15]

Ultimately, greater local participation will depend on the support and encouragement of host governments. Without such support the U.N. system and NGOs are not in as good a position to help forge local participatory mechanisms. This was not a major goal of ICARA II as such. However, as infrastructural projects are evaluated and new ones designed, it will be important to ensure that the needs of the locally affected population, whether refugees or nationals, are being addressed.

SUMMARY

Governments of refugee hosting countries will play a crucial role in the implementation of refugee-related development assistance.

They need to do their utmost to encourage adequate coordination between the donor countries and U.N. agencies so that implementation goes smoothly. They also need to ensure that their own development ministries and refugee agencies have coordinated their respective responsibilities, so that existing projects can be effectively promoted and implemented and new projects can be designed as future needs become known. Working closely with the donors and U.N. system, they need to design ways to ensure that projects can be effectively absorbed. They need to identify technical assistance needs, to determine the extent of recurrent costs, and to factor all of these into the design of projects. Where appropriate, host governments should consult the local population and refugees in areas where refugee-related development projects are likely to be implemented. Finally, if host governments fail to treat refugee-related development assistance as a matter of high priority, it is unlikely that the international community at large will either. As the drought abates, the regeneration of interest in the themes of ICARA II can be hastened if the African governments choose to emphasize them as part of the rehabilitation effort.

NOTES

1. See A/CONF125/2, p. 22, for a breakdown of the projects by sector and country. The amount of resources devoted to infrastructure, as such, can be obtained only by consulting individual project outlines, which usually indicate how much of the indicative cost of the project is devoted to infrastructure.
2. Jacobs and Paar, 'Impact of Urban Refugees.'
3. See UNHCR, *Special Report: Refugee Integration*, passim.
4. See speech by the UNDP Resident Representative in Rwanda at the Conference on African famine in Geneva in March 1985. The sensitivity to the absorptive capacity of the land is the foremost consideration among Rwandan government officials.
5. I am indebted to Lance Clark of the Refugee Policy Group for this insight, which he gained from visits to the field while doing research on a U.S. AID-funded study of well-established refugee settlements.
6. A/CONF.125/2. See also, 'ICARA II: Development Efforts Needed to Aid 4 Million Refugees in Africa,' *U.N. Chronicle*, 21, 6 (1984): 3–11, for a brief country-by-country synopsis of the African submissions.

7. Based on interviews with Somali officials in the Ministry of Planning (Spring 1984).

8. For data on food needs, see FAO Special Report, 'Food Supply Situation in African Countries Affected by Food and Agricultural Emergencies in 1984/1985' 7 December 1984.

9. For example, an Italian mission to Ethiopia had to be cancelled, largely because of the pressing needs on manpower caused by the drought.

10. See the UNHCR annual report to the Executive Committee, A/AC.96/639, 1 August 1984, pp. 83–84, for details on the plans for refugee settlement in Somalia.

11. See Thayer Scudder, 'From Relief to Development: Some Comments on Refugee and Other Settlement in Somalia,' Paper prepared for U.S. AID (June, 1981).

12. For details on the impact of drought in Sudan, see 'Crisis in Sudan,' *Refugees* No. 15 (March 1985): 19–30, and; *Refugees,* no. 16 (April 1985): 9–16.

13. See the joint UNDP/COR document detailing status of ICARA II follow-up. Khartoum, Sudan. This document is revised and updated as required.

14. See, for instance, the report of ICVA consultant given at the General Conference in Dakar, Senegal (May 1985); and the UNHCR Report on Refugee Aid and Development, which is appended to this study as Annex 5.

15. For a statement on the need for greater refugee participation in particular, see the recommendations of the Oxford Symposium Report, 'Assistance to Refugees: Alternative Viewpoints' (Oxford University, Refugee Studies Program, March 1984).

CHAPTER 6

The Role of NGOs

Nongovernmental organizations are newcomers neither to the refugee nor development business. They have been involved for years in both activities, and have developed a generally good reputation in the process. In this chapter, we will review the NGO role in the ICARA II process. We will examine some of the strengths and weaknesses of NGOs, review NGO/U.N. system relations, discuss the NGO role in ICARA II preparation and follow-up, and identify some institutional steps which could be taken to improve NGO involvement in the process.

NGOS AS REFUGEE AND DEVELOPMENT ASSISTANCE VEHICLES

NGOs are a very diverse lot. Some are involved only in relief assistance, others in development.[1] Some do both. Some are very large in size and scope of activity, many are quite small. Their philosophical orientation varies considerably, some being secular, others religious in character. Some are capable of doing large-scale relief or development activities, while others rely on small-scale, grass-roots activity. In short, NGOs are a large and varied reservoir of manpower and expertise. They are an important part of the contemporary international development and relief assistance network.

According to the Organization for Economic Cooperation and Development (OECD) Directory, there are about 1,500 NGOs around the world.[2] Most are found in developed countries but many indigenous voluntary agencies also exist. Several hundred NGOs have consultative status with the United Nations, and in that capacity are an important source of international lobbying for development and humanitarian activities. But a substantial number of NGOs have no direct contact with the U.N. system. As private agencies, neither do most have official ties to governments, although many governments funnel bilateral resources through NGOs to implement specific projects.

NGOs are involved in a wide array of refugee and development assistance programs in virtually every developing country in the world. They address development needs in health, education, technical training, agricultural development, water supply management, sanitation, animal husbandry, reforestation, transportation logistics, program management, and income generation. Some NGOs have expertise in only one or a few of these areas. Some have capabilities in several areas.

As a collectivity, NGOs have rarely accounted for more than 10 percent of the total Official Development Assistance (ODA) provided to developing countries.[3] But much of the assistance they do provide would not otherwise reach developing countries. Moreover, the significance of NGOs in assistance programs should not be measured in monetary terms alone. More important is their contribution to the manpower pool for implementation of assistance projects. In addition, because of their generally small-scale approach, their use of volunteers, and their comparatively low overhead costs, NGOs can often make development and relief resources stretch much further than governments or international organizations. These factors, combined with their access to the grass-roots level in many Third World countries, make NGOs an attractive vehicle for assistance programming.[4]

However, the reputation of NGOs as innovators, promoters of grass-roots development, mobilizers of local participation and as highly cost-effective organizations has been challenged by recent studies.[5] Some evidence suggests that NGOs are less innovative than sometimes claimed. In some cases, NGOs claim to be innovative when instead they have merely expanded or slightly adapted existing development approaches. Similarly, although NGOs claim to be able to mobilize grass-roots participation in development, and to oppose the trickle-down approach of many governments, a closer look at evaluations of projects they have implemented suggests that they often work with local elites as

134

opposed to the poorest of the poor.[6] In other words, they may be engaging in trickle-down strategies at the local level. The claim that NGOs improve grass-roots participation, then, may not be so clear. Similarly, the cost-effectiveness and replicability of NGO development projects has been called into question.[7]

In short, NGOs may not measure up completely to the image they have cultivated. However, short of meeting a standard of perfection, they are probably in a better position than either governments or multilateral organizations to address the development needs of the rural poor. Without their inputs, international development efforts would be hampered. And there is reason to believe that a greater NGO activity – especially with indigenous counterpart agencies – would be beneficial.

NGOS, THE UNITED NATIONS SYSTEM AND ICARA II

Although a number of NGOs have consultative status with the United Nations, the only U.N. agency to use NGOs extensively as implementing partners has been the UNHCR.[8] Through its NGO liaison office and its contacts with the International Council of Voluntary Agencies (ICVA) in Geneva, the UNHCR has built a close relationship with the NGO sector. This has been especially true of NGOs whose primary focus is humanitarian assistance and emergency relief. Ties with development-oriented NGOs have been weaker. However, some NGOs that do both relief and development have strong ties with the UNHCR.

This contrasts sharply with NGO relations with U.N. agencies in the development field. Although NGOs have been involved in a large number of bilaterally funded development programs and in dizzying array of direct people-to-people activities, they have not established close working ties with multilateral development agencies. There are several reasons for this. First the U.N. development agencies have not sought out NGOs as implementing partners, preferring instead to work with other U.N. agencies or host governments. Second, NGOs, have preferred to work on smaller scale projects than those typically funded by the U.N. development agencies. In other words, there has been a lack of fit between NGO program activity and larger scale U.N. system programs. Moreover, many NGOs prefer to use private funds and to steer clear of governmental and intergovernmental development grants. So both the small size and preference of many NGOs has not been conducive to financial links with U.N. agencies. But many are sufficiently large and experienced to be executing partners for such agencies. Many have participated in government-funded development activities. In other words, a number of them would be willing and able to work with U.N. agencies if the institutional mechanisms to facilitate this existed.

ICARA II has provided an opportunity for NGOs and U.N. agencies to initiate new ties. Indeed, in the discussions on refugee aid and development which preceded ICARA II, NGOs played a vocal role. Even before 1980, many had begun to think about the need to move beyond pure relief to development in refugee-impacted areas. But not until ICARA II helped to frame the issues, did the subject increase in visibility.

As preparations for ICARA II proceeded, expectations rose – especially in the UNHCR – that NGOs could and would play a crucial role in mobilizing support for project implementation after the conference. The UNHCR organized numerous Steering committee briefings in Geneva and elsewhere for NGOs.[9] They pointed out to NGOs that roughly a quarter of the ICARA II projects were costed at less than $1 million – a fact that would allow even many of the smaller agencies to consider taking an implementation role or partially funding projects in coordination with other agencies.

If there was considerable expectation among relevant IOs that NGOs should be drawn actively into the ICARA II process, not all NGOs were equally excited about joining forces with the UNDP. As noted frequently above, the donors had strongly urged and the U.N. system had decided that the UNDP should play the lead role in addressing 5c programs. But, for a variety of reasons, NGOs (particularly those headquartered in Geneva) were opposed to a lead role for the UNDP. They preferred instead that the UNHCR be called on to play this role. This sentiment was underscored in the ICVA statement to ICARA II:

> The participation of the [UNDP] in the Conference's Steering committee and its role in preparing the projects outlines are welcomed. However, this must

not be allowed to detract from the paramount role of the [UNHCR] in the field of assistance to refugees, whether the projects are funded through his Office or through other U.N. agencies. While UNDP may have a role to play in the follow-up to 5c projects, we believe that UNHCR still has the overall responsibility in this area as well.[10]

Stubborn adherence to this view demonstrated that many of the NGOs were, at least in this respect, out of step with the main thrust of ICARA II.

As noted above, NGOs have worked closely with the UNHCR as implementors of emergency assistance, resettlement and returnee programs. On the other hand, they have not worked with the UNDP. It is understandable that NGOs would prefer to work with a known quantity: their traditional ties with the UNHCR explain a good deal of their reluctance to work with the UNDP. Beyond this underlying motivation, several arguments were advanced by NGOs to support a lead role for the UNHCR rather than the UNDP.

First, some vocal voices in the NGO community pointed out that the UNDP was unlikely to have sufficient resources to respond to the 5c projects. They accurately pointed out that the UNDP had been under financial constraints in the early 1980s, owing to decreasing revenues.[11] Moreover, the UNDP had no additional resources for ICARA II, and, as some NGOs saw it, were unlikely to be provided resources for ICARA II by donors. As they saw it, most of the resources would be provided through bilateral channels. In several respects this view of the UNDP resource situation was not inaccurate. The UNDP had some difficult years in the early 1980s, but has since recovered somewhat. It is true, too, that most of the donor countries will pursue bilateral responses to ICARA II. However, some NGOs miscalculated the desire of donor countries to ensure not only a key UNDP role in monitoring 5c activities, but to bolster this with contributions to UNDP trust fund arrangements.

Apart from the financial considerations, some NGO officials objected to what they viewed as the artificial split between 5b and 5c projects.[12] Some felt this division would not be in the best interests of refugees. Since the UNHCR has the mandate for reaching durable solutions for refugees, some of these NGO officials felt that the UNHCR should handle both the 5b and 5c projects, with the UNDP playing only an ancillary role. What this view failed to take into account was that the 5c projects were meant less to be assistance to refugees than to the host governments so that the latter could address the infrastructural needs in refugee-affected regions. Although no one would deny that there is overlap between the 5b and 5c concepts, especially in the case of refugee settlement activities, on the whole the 5c projects are clearly more developmental in nature. As such, they fall within the purview of the UNDP, not the UNHCR. Such, at least, was the view of the donor community, which was unwilling to entertain an expansion of the UNHCR mandate into this more clearly developmental activity.[13]

It should be noted at this point, that NGO attitudes about the role of the UNDP versus UNHCR were not uniform. Some vocal and influential organizations in Geneva prevailed when it came to drafting the pro-UNHCR stance announced by ICVA at ICARA II. But many NGOs did not share the same degree of opposition to a lead role for the UNDP. If nothing else, the ICVA stance served notice to UNDP that it had a good deal of public relations work to accomplish before effective linkages could be established with the NGO sector. These efforts continue to this day.

NGO ACTIVITIES SINCE ICARA II

In some respects expectations about the celerity and potency of the NGO response to ICARA II implementation were higher than they should have been. High expectations for NGOs were shared not only by UNHCR officials but by knowledgeable commentators on the relief and development process as well. Mark Malloch Brown, editor of the Economist's *Development Review,* went so far as to declare that NGOs were the big winners at ICARA II, and the UNDP the big loser.[14] In this view, the NGOs – which had not actively sought a major role in ICARA II – danced away with most of the donor attention and money, leaving the major U.N. agencies, chiefly the UNDP, playing the role of the wallflower. There is little doubt that the nearly 100 NGOs which attended ICARA II, felt a sense of euphoria at their apparent success there. Many kind words were said about the vitality and appropriateness of NGO assistance in the emerging field of refugee aid and development. But a closer look at what happened at ICARA II suggests neither that UNDP was a big loser nor that NGOs walked away with a clear-cut triumph.[15]

While it is true that NGOs are a natural constituency for the philosophical approach embodied in the ICARA II projects, their actual capacity to carry forward implementation expeditiously was and is limited. Probably the single most influential factor limiting an aggressive response by NGOs was the lack of readily available resources. Despite announced intentions by many donors to make use of NGOs as implementing partners, very little hard cash was actually available in the immediate aftermath of ICARA II. Without an additional source of funds, most NGOs simply are not in a position to commit themselves to implementation of specific projects. Their capacity to raise money in the private sector for large-scale development projects is limited. Resources for such projects are usually sought from governments or international agencies. The resource dilemma was rectified to a certain extent by the overwhelming public response to the African famine in late 1985 and early 1986. Many NGOs collected unusually large amounts of contributions during that period – some $110 million in the United States alone.[16] However, the majority of these resources were designated for emergency relief activities rather than for long-term development. Still, many NGOs have more change jingling around today for discretionary programs. They should be giving ICARA II-related projects – and not necessarily only those presented at the conference – a close look.

A second factor – related to the first – was that some confusion existed among NGOs about how they should proceed. Many NGOs found themselves waiting to see how the U.N. system would act and whether donor countries would commit themselves to particular projects. Many NGOs adopted this wait-and-see strategy, hoping to get a better feel in the months after ICARA II about how they fit into the larger picture. Some NGOs have taken the attitude that they need to be persuaded by governments or the U.N. agencies to give a higher priority to ICARA II projects instead of other activities in which they are currently engaged. Some are skeptical that ICARA II should be given a high priority when balanced against other needs. Should this view gain ascendency among NGOs, it is clear that ICARA II would suffer. Indeed a more constructive response would be for NGOs to fashion their own approach to meeting ICARA II needs and actively promote it. They need not, in other words, sit back and passively wait to be persuaded.

If the NGOs, as a group, have not responded with the kind of aggressiveness many in the UNHCR had hoped they would, their degree of passivity has varied. To understand these degrees of passivity, it is necessary to consider the different circumstances facing NGOs in Europe and the United States.

On the European side of the Atlantic, NGOs have been better informed and more involved in both preparations for and follow-up to ICARA II. In large part this can be explained by the fact that ICVA is headquartered in Geneva. Although ICVA's membership includes a large number of American, as well as European, NGOs, most of the former do not have permanent representation in Geneva. On the whole, then, European NGOs were more actively and directly engaged in response to ICARA II than their American counterparts. Even before ICARA II, ICVA had begun the process of reviewing the project documentation in order to identify projects most suitable for NGO involvement. On 26 April 1984, ICVA's Sub-group on African Refugees decided that an independent assessment by NGOs was necessary. One special meeting of the Sub-group met prior to ICARA II to discuss the submission of Sudan.[17] Four subsequent sessions spanning the six months after ICARA II were held at Oxford, Brussels and Geneva to study the submissions of the other African countries. Initially, it was ICVA's intention to release each of the reviews as they were completed on a country-by-country basis. However, as the reviews progressed it became clear to the technical experts involved that many of the project concepts either were not feasible or required substantial revision to be workable. Only a small inventory of projects would be immediately suitable for NGO implementation. ICVA decided that a general final report should be issued rather than the unedited versions of each country submission evaluation. The latter were apparently sufficiently candid to have potentially offended some host countries. In any case, the results of these studies were contained in a report which was submitted at the ICVA General Conference Meetings at Dakar, Senegal in May 1985. This report was authored by David De Pury, who had been retained by ICVA as a consultant in the fall of 1984 to coordinate its follow-through efforts on ICARA II and to act as a focal point for ICVA contacts with UNHCR and UNDP.[18]

The above-mentioned steps taken by ICVA illustrate the importance it attached to ICARA II. However, the impulse to study has not been matched everywhere by an aggressive approach to securing funding for projects. As of the end of 1984, only a few European NGOs were in active consultations with governments about implementation of ICARA II projects (See Table 6.1).[19] Moreover, although the study process was meant to encourage NGO consortia and joint efforts, none was in the offing as 1985 began.

For U.N. officials who had hoped to see NGOs dynamically setting the pace after ICARA II, and actively moving governments to action, the European NGOs response was disappointing. A number of donor governments had stipulated they would work through NGOs in responding to ICARA II. The U.K. went so far as to earmark its $6 million contribution announced at ICARA II for use by NGOs.[20] But there was no stampede by NGOs to secure these or other available funds. Admittedly, the amounts of readily available additional resources were initially small. But this need not have prevented NGOs from approaching governments or the UNDP directly to discuss financing alternatives for projects they found attractive. In other words, while European NGOs have been ready to study the project concepts, they have been less aggressive in identifying project alternatives where existing projects have been found wanting, and in following up with potential donors those projects that seem promising.

By comparison, American NGOs have been even more passive in their response to ICARA II. Several factors explain this. First, as mentioned above, American NGOs are not as actively plugged into the Geneva-based activities of ICVA as are their European counterparts. Fewer ICARA II public relations activities took place in the United States. The Refugee Policy Group (RPG) sponsored sessions in Washington, D.C. on the occasion of the Steering Committee's visit for discussions with the U.S. government (a briefing for NGOs was also held in New York on the same Steering Committee trip). The RPG later sponsored a symposium/briefing on ICARA II which attracted some NGO participation and interest in April of 1984.[21] This contrasts with the almost continuous contact ICVA maintained with the UNHCR ICARA II unit and the numerous briefings held by the Steering Committee for NGOs in Geneva.

Compounding this problem was the fact that the American NGOs were in the throes of a reorganization involving the American Council for Voluntary Agencies (ACVA) and Private Agencies In Development (PAID). These agencies operated as overall coordinating mechanisms for American NGOs. Although they collaborated extensively before 1984, a decision was taken in that year to merge the two organizations, so that their coordination efforts could be streamlined. The merger and the negotiations leading up to it drew considerable attention from NGOs in the months following ICARA II. Once the merger was effected in October of 1984, the new umbrella organization, now called Interaction, was faced with the task of consolidating its programs. It had little time to devote to ICARA II then. In other words, lacking any overall leadership regarding ICARA II, U.S. NGOs were left to their own devices and initiative. Unlike the European case, no NGO review of the ICARA II submissions took place and, other than a few joint UNDP/UNHCR briefings in New York, little was done to ensure that ICARA II would remain a visible priority in the American NGO community at large.

Finally, many American and European NGOs, found their immediate energies turning toward the massive African drought relief effort. While the public response in the Western world to the famine left the coffers of many NGOs brimming with new money, most of it was earmarked for the emergency. Moreover, most NGOs found themselves barely able to keep pace with the emergency needs, let alone think about significant expansion of ICARA II and other development-related programs. The organizational capacity of some NGOs to absorb and to effectively spend all of the famine-related resources while simultaneously addressing ICARA II has been limited. Whatever attention might otherwise have been devoted to ICARA II, was quickly diverted to meeting emergency relief needs.

Despite the lack of a concerted and centralized effort to promote U.S. NGO response to ICARA II, some individual NGOs have sought a concrete role. Africare, for instance, began implementation of the U.S.-funded Nasho Cattle Ranch project in Rwanda. The United States also funded an ICARA II Aguaculture project in Zambia with the International Catholic Migration Commission (ICMC). The possibility for other NGOs to become actively involved still exists. They do not need to wait for either the U.S. government or the UNDP to seek opportunities out. Rather, they could be more active in promoting ICARA II projects and seeking funding for them – an approach that has been sadly lacking in both Europe and the United States.

Nevertheless, NGOs continue to show interest in some ICARA II projects. Some projects are actually being implemented by them and others are under active consideration. Table 6.1 summarizes the current status of ICARA II activity by NGOs. As the Table shows, fifteen projects are at least under study at this time and four of them are actually under implementation. Although the projects under study may not in every case be implemented, Table 6.1 suggests that a few NGOs (certainly not as large a number as one might like to see actively involved) have shown some initial interest and that they could play a significant part in the successful implementation of the ICARA II process. The challenge will be to get a larger number of NGOs involved in ICARA II follow-up, and to get them thinking creatively about how to meet ICARA II-related needs in ways that are commensurate with traditional NGO values and priorities.

INSTITUTIONAL NEEDS

Ideally, NGOs should perform three major functions in ICARA II follow-up, including implementation, promotion and identification/evaluation of 5c projects. To date, NGOs have perceived themselves as implementors and to a lesser extent evaluators of these projects. However, they have not yet promoted 5c projects to any significant degree, nor have they identified additional projects which would address ICARA II objectives.

Table 6.1. NGO interest in ICARA II infrastructural projects.

Country	Project/Sector	NGO(s)	Status
Angola	School Construction	World University Service (WUS) (International and Denmark)	Feasibility study conducted March/April 1985 with Euro-Action Accord (EAA)
	Establishment of 6 community development centers	EAA (partial project)	Feasibility Study, April/May 1985 with WUS
Botswana	Health Screening	WUS (Canada)	Implementation with CIDA support likely
Kenya	Vocational Training Center	YMCA (Kenya)	Under Implementation with Norway funding
Rwanda	Nasho Cattle Ranch	Africare	Under Implementation
	Craft Training Centers	Caritas	Under Implementation with Cor Unum and Miseror support
	Reintegration of Returnees	EAA (partial project)	Under Study
	Primary Schools (Rukomo)	EAA (partial project)	Under Study
	Community Centers	EAA (partial project)	Under Study
Sudan	Red Sea Health	EAA/WUS (Canada), et. al.	Under Study
	South, Teacher Training	WUS (UK)	Possible Interest
	South, Vocational Training	Norwegian Church Aid	Interest if Norwegian government funds available
Zaire	Health in Aru, Cataractes, Shaba	Association Internationale du Developpement Rural (AIDR) and Methodist Church	Under Implementation with Dutch and U.S. AID funding
	Water Rehabilitation	AIDR	Under Implementation with U.S. AID Funding
Zambia	Aquaculture	International Catholic Migration Commission	Under Implementation with U.S. Funding

Several problems, many of which are shared with U.N. agencies and governments, must be addressed if NGOs hope to contribute their full potential to the ICARA II process. The first of these problems concerns the relationship between NGO headquarters and their field offices, regarding respective roles for ICARA II.

Although most NGO officials understood the basic themes of ICARA II, this understanding did not always extend to field representatives. Indeed, NGO field representatives tend to be of variable quality, and there is often a great deal of turnover in these posts. Yet, as far as future program development is concerned, NGO field staff will be the linchpins of eventual success. They are in a position to identify small-scale projects to address refugee-related development burdens. They are best qualified to assess how NGOs could contribute to existing project proposals. They will implement the projects. Indeed, they are the ones who should be undertaking review of the ICARA II submissions. Headquarters review of these projects are important, too. But these need to be bolstered by adequate field participation, to ensure realistic assessment.

NGOs have a long way to go before their field representatives are apprised of the nature of ICARA II and the key role they will play in the NGO response. In part this problem is a function of the general lack of visibility from which ICARA II has suffered, especially in light of the current drought. This is all the more reason NGOs should do their utmost to ensure that ICARA II themes are made a matter of priority. Four key points should be stressed here.

First, field representatives should be encouraged to evaluate the existing ICARA II proposals in order to assess potential roles for their organizations. Second, they should be encouraged to look beyond the existing ICARA II project proposals, to identify other refugee-related development needs, which they might be in a better position to address. There is no reason why NGOs must adhere slavishly to the existing list of projects. In fact, they would do a major service by finding scaled down versions of the ICARA II projects. Infrastructure need not always be large-scale in scope. More NGOs might be in a position to contribute to the process of meeting refugee-related development burdens if smaller scale projects were identified. They need only take the ICARA II concept and think in somewhat more modest terms. No doubt literally dozens of project opportunities could be generated if NGOs would only refocus their ICARA II efforts in a way that befits their traditional small-scale approach. Third, where projects are appealing but perhaps too ambitious in scope for a single agency, consideration should be given to partnerships or consortia with other NGOs. Finally, NGO headquarters must take the ultimate responsibility for ensuring the visibility of ICARA II. They need to direct their field representatives to keep their eyes open for opportunities.

Many of these points were underscored in the recommendations of the ICVA Consultant's Report on ICARA II. The report stressed, for example, the need for NGOs to review the ICARA projects and to determine how they might contribute to implementation of parts or all of particular projects. The report also underscored the importance of the field representatives in this process. To give NGO participation a boost in the field, the ICVA consultant made trips to Zaire, Ethiopia, Somalia and Uganda to meet with NGO representatives and relevant U.N. and government officials. He recommended that ICVA should invite a lead agency in each of the chief host countries to promote informally NGO liaison and collaboration on infrastructure projects – a suggestion which has considerable merit and which is under serious consideration in several countries.[22]

A second major problem facing NGO involvement in ICARA II concerns the bifurcation that has developed between the European and American response. Too little communication has existed between European NGOs who have at least conducted extensive reviews of ICARA II projects and American NGOs, who are as, a general rule, still waiting around to see what will happen. ICVA and Interaction should make every effort to ensure the free flow of information on ICARA II. Lessons learned from the European review exercise should be shared fully with American NGOs. In the meantime both ICVA and Interaction should make ICARA II follow-up a matter of priority concern for its membership.

ICVA, in fact, appears ready to continue its stewardship of ICARA promotion. The consultant's report recommended that

ICVA should continue its role as focal point and information clearinghouse for member agencies so long as they believe is necessary. In addition, the consultant has been retained to work with the smaller agencies which thus far have not been centrally involved in ICARA II follow-up. The objective of this work is to help the smaller agencies identify components of existing projects or ancillary projects which promote ICARA II infrastructural objectives.[23]

A third problem concerns NGO relations with the UNDP. As noted above, UNDP/NGO relations have been problematical for a variety of reasons. The UNDP has taken steps to assure NGOs of its desire to establish broader ties, although often NGO officials have interpreted the UNDP style as being somewhat heavy-handed. Nevertheless, NGOs should make every effort to work more closely with UNDP. One area in which they could test a new relationship would be to conduct joint feasibility studies of potentially promising projects. After several years of evaluating its relationship to the NGO sector, the UNDP has developed financial mechanisms to make joint feasibility studies and programming with NGOs possible.[24] Depending on the result of such studies, NGOs could negotiate financial arrangements between UNDP and donor governments to implement selected projects. On this subject and others, the UNDP ICARA II follow-up unit is now at least in communication with ICVA. However, periodic communication is one thing and active collaboration another. The latter has yet to be achieved but is sorely needed.

Finally, NGOs have an important advocacy role to play in ICARA II follow-up. Philosophically they should continue to insist that refugee aid and development assistance be treated as related activities. Practically speaking, they should be urging donor country legislatures to appropriate additional refugee-related development resources. Similarly, they should play a greater role in promoting funding for specific projects. Some NGOs have mounted significant advocacy efforts. In the U.K., for instance, the British Refugee Council was quite vocal in support of ICARA II before the conference took place.[25] Not coincidentally, the British government announced that its contribution would be channelled through NGOs and has developed a set of guidelines for them to follow in preparing project proposals.[26] In addition, a small number of American NGOs lobbied actively, if unsuccessfully, for inclusion of substantial resources for ICARA II in the emergency drought appropriations considered by the U.S. Congress.[27] These efforts are to be commended. But the task is a continuous one in which a broader range of NGOs should be involved. NGOs need to keep the donor's feet to the fire and to press them to respond favorably to the refugee-related development needs that were so central to the work of ICARA II.

In the meantime, they need to think more creatively about how to leverage the resources raised during Africa's recent emergency into longer-term development projects. They also need to identify smaller-scale projects with ICARA II implications. Even more specifically, they may be better placed than other entities to identify specific burdens borne by host country nationals – burdens which are not always remediable through the application of large-scale infrastructural projects. NGOs are in a position, in other words, to remind their governmental and intergovernmental colleagues that the real burdens in refugee-impacted areas are often borne directly on the shoulders of the local people. NGOs, working with indigenous groups, could serve a useful function by ensuring that the voices of the host population and of the refugees are heard as governments define and address refugee-related development burdens.

NOTES

1. For a wide-ranging discussion of both the relief and development activities of NGOs see John Sommer, *Beyond Charity: U.S. Voluntary Aid for A Changing World* (Washington, D.C.: Overseas Development Council, 1977); Landrum Bolling and Craig Smith, *Private Foreign Aid: U.S. Philanthropy for Relief and Development* (Boulder, CO: Westview Press, 1982), and; Jorgen Lissner, The Politics of Altruism: A study of the Political Behavior of Voluntary Development Agencies (Geneva: Lutheran World Federation, 1977). A number of useful case studies of NGO relief and development activities can also be cited; Mervyn Jones, *In Famine's Shadow: A Private War on Hunger* (Boston: Beacon Press, 1965); Eugene Linden, *The Alms Race: The Impact of American Voluntary Aid Abroad* (New York: Random House, 1976), and; David Forsythe, *Humanitarian Politics: The International Committee of the Red Cross* (Baltimore, MD: Johns Hopkins Univer-

sity Press, 1977). For a specific treatment of NGO activity in refugee assistance, see, Robert Gorman, 'Private Voluntary Organizations in Refugee Relief', In Elizabeth Ferris, *Refugees in World Politics* (New York: Praeger, 1985).

2. OECD, *Directory of Non-governmental Organizations in OECD Member Countries Active in Development Cooperation,* v. 1, (Paris, 1981).
3. See Robert F. Gorman, ed., *Private Voluntary Organizations as Agents of Development* (Boulder, CO: Westview Press, 1984), pp. 51–55.
4. See Elliott Schwartz, *Private Voluntary Organizations in Development in Foreign Aid* (Washington, D.C.: Office of Management and Budget, 1976).
5. See Judith Tendler, *Turning Voluntary Organizations into Development Agencies: Questions for Evaluation,* Evaluation Discussion Paper No. 12, (Washington, D.C.: AID, 1982).
6. *Ibid.,* pp. 11–33.
7. See Gene Ellis, 'Making PVOs Count More: A Proposal,' in Robert F. Gorman, ed., *Private Voluntary Organizations as Agents of Development,* pp. 201–213.
8. The UNHCR has a very active NGO Liaison Unit and well-developed guidelines on NGO participation as implementors of UNHCR refugee assistance programs.
9. In addition to the Geneva briefings for NGOs, the Steering Committee conducted NGO workshops in New York, Ottawa, Canberra and Tokyo; See *ICVA News,* no. 105 (Geneva: May 1984), p. 1.
10. See ICVA Statement to ICARA II, July 9–11, 1984, p. 2.
11. See *supra,* Chapter 3 note 3.
12. Based on interviews with NGO officials in Geneva, November, 1984.
13. For a balanced discussion of NGO views on relations with UNHCR and UNDP, as well as a treatment of UNHCR/UNDP relations see; Barber, 'Voluntary Agency Perspectives.'
14. Mark Malloch Brown, 'The Rise and Rise of the Volag,' *The Development Report* (August, 1984), pp. 1–2.
15. *Ibid.*
16. See the Interfaith Action for Economic Justice Policy Notes Note 85–5 (April 4, 1985), p. 5 for figures on famine-related contribution levels.
17. *ICVA News,* No. 106, (Geneva, July 1984), p. 2.
18. See David DePury, 'Report to ICVA on ICARA II Follow-up,' paper delivered at the ICVA General Conference, Dakar, Senegal, May 1985.
19. Based on interviews with NGO and government officials in Geneva and London, November 1984.
20. See UK statement to ICARA II, July 9–11, 1984, Geneva, Switzerland.
21. For a summary of this meeting see: 'Refugee Policy Group,' ICARA II: Future Directions for Assistance to Refugees in Africa' (Washington, D.C.: 1984).
22. DePury, 'Report on ICARA II,' pp. 14–15.
23. *Ibid.,* p. 15.
24. See UNDP, *Note on Procedures for Contracting with NGOs* (New York, 1985).

25. In addition to a series of informative briefings papers on ICARA II, the British Refugee Council published a Policy statement calling for the British government to support the basic themes of ICARA II. See, British Refugee Council, *Africa's Refugee Crisis: New Directions for Assistance, Aid and Development* (June 1984).

26. British officials admit that the NGO lobby was instrumental in its decision to provide resources for ICARA II through the voluntary sector. They also stress that the government believes that NGOs are best placed in Africa to address the refugee-related development focus called for in the ICARA II projects. The guidelines stress, among other things, that NGO projects should be realistic, attainable, administratively viable and based on clearly defined costs.

27. The budget situation in the U.S. Congress regarding ICARA II is described above in Chapter 4. It is important to note here, however, that without the efforts of a few NGOs, funds for ICARA II might well have been left completely out of the second version of the Weiss-Wolpe bill. Unfortunately, they were not sufficiently influential to ensure that the $ 50 million proposed in the first Weiss-Wolpe bill was retained throughout the entire legislative process.

PART THREE

Future Directions

CHAPTER 7

Moving beyond ICARA II

Over the past few years the international community witnessed the deterioration of the African environment with increasing alarm. Images of a desiccated continent, of emaciated people and dying herds of livestock became commonplace. Development specialists and relief workers whispered about the drought as a harbinger of the wholesale environmental degradation of the continent. Africa was likened to the dustbowl in the American mid-west during the Great Depression.[1] Pessimistic forecasts and prophecies of gloom grew in frequency. Some even referred to the widespread African famine – in which tens, perhaps hundreds, of thousands of people perished – as a holocaust. Only rarely through these saturnine predictions and dark images has any optimism been apparent.[2] Indeed, recent developments have underscored the formidable problems Africa will face in future years. But sober reflection on what could be happening in Africa should not lead us to a fatalistic passivity. Rather, these daunting problems should be treated as a call to action. Nor should it be assumed that prospects for development are everywhere so bleak, or that where they are now bleak that they shall ever be so. Africa poses a great challenge, but it also holds great potential. Indeed, the return of the rains in several drought-stricken countries has brought with it new hope.

The international community as a whole has shown renewed determination to grapple with Africa's emergency and long-term development needs. Private initiatives such as the Live Aid concert and numerous similar efforts have awakened the world to the tremendous needs in Africa. Nor have public international agencies been inactive. To cope with the African emergency, the

Secretary-General announced the creation of UNOEOA (UN Office for Emergency Operations in Africa) in December of 1984. In the meantime, meetings of other UN bodies and the OAU focused attention on the longer term development issues that transcended the emergency. In July 1984, at the 13th FAO Regional Conference on Africa, the Harare Declaration on the African food crisis underscored the importance of achieving agricultural self-sufficiency in Africa. A year later the OAU adopted a Priority Programme for Africa's economic recovery which emphasized the primary responsibility of African countries for their own development.[3] This Priority Programme later served as the basis for discussions at the General Assembly's special session on African Economic Recovery and Development, which marked the first time a special session ever has been devoted to a regional concern.[4] This special session was held in May of 1986.

The refugee problem was not the central concern of this special meeting, but it was at least included on the agenda. Moreover, the UN Programme of Action for African Economic Recovery and Development 1986–1990 is replete with proposals for emergency preparedness, agricultural rehabilitation, land reclamation and human resource development, which are as applicable in refugee-affected regions as they are in other parts of the continent. The Programme of Action also reiterated the basic themes of ICARA II and called for an acceleration of implementation of its recommendations.[5] Although only a few countries explicitly addressed or mentioned the refugee issue or ICARA II during the special session debate, the basic thrust of the discussion was clearly in keeping with the themes that dominated discussions at ICARA II, including the need for better coordination of assistance, a desire to work within existing institutional mechanisms, the recognition that Africa must undertake seriously to resolve its problems and that the international community should assist the Africans by providing resources to bolster these endeavors.

Set against this backdrop, ICARA II should be viewed as but one, and at that a rather modest, part of the international response to African relief and development needs. It is but one of many roads that could be followed to improve the lot of African countries hosting refugees. Its theme was a simple and attractive one which for a time at least has drawn refugee and development specialists into a dialogue on how effectively to link assistance activities in the two fields. Much of the forgoing has focused on how governments and assistance agencies have responded to this challenge. The question that arises is whether ICARA II and the larger process of fostering linkages between refugee and development assistance have been and will be a success.

MEASURING SUCCESS

Although it is premature to make final judgments about the success of ICARA II and the linkage of refugee aid and development, several general observations can be made about current trends. But first it is important to make a distinction between the theoretical or philosophical and the practical achievements of ICARA II.

Philosophical Achievements

On the philosophical side of the ledger, it would seem that ICARA II sharpened and focused an already emerging dialogue on the connections between refugees and development. It led to a consensus regarding the need to help asylum countries cope with additional burdens placed on their economic infrastructure by refugees. Some argument still exists about the exact nature of the burden and how to address it, but there is widespread agreement that the refugee-related burden is real and that it should be addressed through developmentally sound assistance. The refugee and development communities are in more direct communication, and the subject of refugee aid and development has become the focus of much more extensive academic inquiry and governmental concern. The result of these discussions, which ICARA II helped to advance, is a logic which can be summarized as follows:

1. The plight of refugees should be addressed through durable solutions at the earliest possible time.
2. Where traditional long-term solutions such as voluntary repatriation, local settlement or third country resettlement are

not immediately feasible, assistance to refugees should encourage productive self-reliance.

3. Promotion of self-reliance and durable solutions often requires attention to the entire area in which refugees reside, especially where land and water resources and employment opportunities are scarce.

4. Assistance to refugees, whether for self-reliance activities or in promotion of voluntary repatriation and local settlement, should take into account the needs of the local population.

5. Refugees place burdens on the economic and social infrastructure of areas in which they reside. These regional burdens are not addressed by traditional direct assistance to the refugees, particularly where refugees are spontaneously settled and beyond the reach of international assistance.

6. Host countries should not be expected to absorb the entire cost of meeting refugee-related development burdens from their regular development programs. The international community should provide some additional resources to meet these additional burdens that have been incurred by the host countries as a result of their generous policies of asylum.

7. Large-scale infrastructure and income generation programs in refugee-affected areas will require a closer linkage between refugee and development programming. This calls for greater cooperation between refugee and development agencies at every level.[6]

If the goals of ICARA II and the basic themes of the refugee aid and development dialogue are reasonably straightforward, there is nevertheless a good deal more that needs to be done if they are to move beyond the realm of philosophy and concept. An important consideration here is that the broader development community – that is beyond the small circle of refugee specialists who have led the inquiry into the connections between refugees and development – must have an increased awareness of and concern about these goals and themes. One should remember that the impetus for discussions on refugee aid and development issues has been provided by refugee agencies like the UNHCR. Similarly, scholars in the field of refugee studies have carried the standard in this area rather than their colleagues in development studies. If the refugee advocates have been primarily responsible for the initiation of the conceptual inquiry into linkages between refugee aid and development and for the genesis of the ICARA process, the advocates and agencies for development can ensure the ultimate success of this effort. But there is still far less awareness in the development community at large about the relationship between refugees and development than in the refugee affairs community. Refugees have occupied a rather peripheral place in the long list of traditional concerns with which development specialists grapple. There is much to be done in order to engage the development community more fully into the process of linking refugee aid and development assistance.

In short, although much progress has been made on the philosophical side of the ICARA II process, especially in promoting a dialogue between development and refugee specialists, the dialogue – or perhaps it would be more accurate to say the educational process – must be broadened and deepened before one can say with confidence that it has succeeded. Moreover, any judgment about the success of the dialogue must ultimately rest on the success of its ends, namely, implementation of development projects which alleviate the refugee burden in developing countries and promote the integration of refugees into the meaningful economic life of their host countries. In other words, it is time for the refugee aid and development debate to move from the halls of government and academia into the practical realm. ICARA II has provided an opportunity for the international community to do this. It is appropriate then, that we next discuss several measures which might be used to gauge the practical as opposed to the philosophical success of the ICARA process.

Practical Achievements

Ultimately, the success of ICARA II as measured in practical terms boils down to the implementation of projects which alleviate the refugee burden on economic and social infrastructure of asylum countries. The ability to accomplish this depends on the availability of resources and the development of institutional capacities and policies among the relevant actors. Before turning to a detailed examination of the major policy questions facing the international community, let us review briefly the resource dimension.

ICARA II initially garnered $ 55 million in pledges from donor countries for infrastructural projects. Since ICARA II several donors that did not make pledges have kicked in another $ 25 million or so, and the European Economic Community has allocated an additional $ 70 million for refugee assistance to the African, Caribbean and Pacific (ACP) countries over the next five years – the lion's share of which will be targeted on African countries with significant infrastructural burdens. Despite this reasonably encouraging start, implementation of the projects has been very slow. As of February 1986, only a handful were actually under implementation, but more than thirty had received a commitment of at least partial funding, (at latest count commitments to fund all or part of about 36 projects have been announced). This adds up to a respectable response for the first few years, when one considers both the slower pace that characterizes development programming of this sort and the chilling effect that the African drought and famine had on ICARA II follow-up. About half of the total of projects presented at ICARA II could be funded in five years, if only a dozen of them can be implemented annually. This is a realistically attainable goal, although it may fall short of African expectations. The UNDP, itself, has funded projects in Djibouti and Lesotho, and is studying projects in Chad and the Central African Republic and other countries that have attracted little donor support for their ICARA II projects.

More important than the actual number of projects funded, will be the fact that refugee-related development projects are given routine consideration in the years to come. If after five years they are still attracting donor interest, then the process established by ICARA II will have achieved one of its major goals – the institutionalization of this new window of assistance. This institutional success will in turn depend not only on the availability of resources but on important policy considerations.

THE POLICY DIMENSION: RECOMMENDATIONS

The international community had two choices regarding how to implement the goals of ICARA II. One would have been to develop a highly visible and centralized bureaucratic structure emphasizing a multilateral assistance approach. For better or worse, this approach was discarded in favor of a more decentralized one which has placed greater emphasis on existing programming mechanisms and on bilateral relationships between the host and donor countries. If the Africans might have preferred the former approach as a way to increase the visibility of their needs and the accountability of donors, the donors would have opposed it. They preferred the decentralized approach which provided them with greater flexibility and discretion in providing assistance.

The decentralized approach was adopted less by conscious choice than by natural evolution. While donors use primarily multilateral channels for their humanitarian aid, most of their development funds are channelled bilaterally. Although ICARA II had definite humanitarian overtones, its primary focus was on development. It was natural, then, that a decentralized approach would find favor with the donors. Nor were the U.N. agencies interested in creating new or elaborate centralized aid mechanisms. It seemed logical, then, that the existing structures for development and refugee programming needed only to be fine tuned in order to accommodate implementation of ICARA II projects.

But the chief advantage of the decentralized approach – i.e., that it exploits existing mechanisms for development planning without adding new, unnecessary and expensive layers of bureaucracy – also places a premium on the need for coordination among the relevant actors, most particularly, but not exclusively, in each of the affected host countries.

The decentralized approach makes monitoring, promotion and evaluation of the ICARA II programs more difficult. It also makes meaningful participation of the beneficiary populations more problematical. Despite its obvious advantages, then, the decentralized approach is a major source of many of the problems that have complicated successful follow-through on ICARA II. Still this approach is politically the most realistic and there are ways to make it work if the relevant actors choose to make it do so.

In the following pages the problems of coordinating, promoting, evaluating and encouraging beneficiary participation in this decentralized context are examined and policy recommendations which would address these problems are proferred.

Coordination

Throughout this book, the issue of coordination has been identified as one of the most essential ingredients to successful ICARA II follow-up. The need for coordination applies to virtually all of the relevant actors, that is, the U.N. system, governments, and NGOs.

There are two related and crucial focal points for coordination: in the individual host countries, themselves, and at the headquarters level in the U.N. system (especially in UNDP), and the donor community. The common thread in this coordination process is the UNDP, which has been authorized to monitor ICARA II follow-up on the infrastructural projects both through its offices in New York and through its resident representatives who will in most cases take the lead in coordinating the international response in each of the affected host countries. The success of the infrastructural projects will rest to a great extent on the style and the substance of the UNDP response.

In the field, the UNDP resident representatives need to exercise energetic but sensitive leadership in keeping track of donor and NGO activities and maximizing the fit between these and the priorities of the host government. In some countries the UNDP representative may play the lead role. In others it may be more appropriate to allow for a larger UNHCR role. At a minimum the UNDP and UNHCR representatives must be in frequent communication. The coordination role of the UNDP resident representatives in each host country is a delicate task. For instance, donors and NGOs often resist being 'coordinated,' nor do they care to submit 'required' reports on the status of their activities to U.N. agencies. The style of coordination, then, must be carefully considered. Ideally, the resident representatives should establish an informal climate of information sharing so that all parties may feel free to communicate the status of their own activities in the interest of learning what others are doing in refugee-affected areas. Where circumstances in the country permit, more formal arrangements could be instituted to encourage comprehensive development strategies for refugee-affected areas. Again, where cirmcumstances allow, the UNDP representatives could use the existing roundtable formats to ensure that refugee-related development needs are addressed. This, in turn, will depend on the desire of the host countries to include the refugee element on its development agenda.

If UNDP coordination within host countries is crucial, the health of ICARA II follow-up also depends to a lesser extent on effective coordination at the headquarters level in the donor community. An important element of this coordination is the information clearinghouse function which is entrusted to the ICARA II unit of UNDP. This function is at the same time more necessary and difficult to accomplish in a decentralized context. Speedy collection and dissemination of information about the activities of the many bilateral responses by donors and NGOs to ICARA II projects has not been, nor will it be, easily achieved. One problem that has hampered the clearinghouse function has been the UNDP proclivity to use the resident representatives in the field as the primary conduit for communication with donor and host countries. In many cases this is the preferable approach. But when the representatives are overwhelmed with emergency related activities, communication can be delayed or impaired. Moreover, information provided by donors to the UNDP representatives in the field and vice-versa, may fail to be reported to their respective headquarters. Confirmation that information has been received and accurately interpreted requires not just headquarter-to-field and field-to-field communication, but also headquarter-to-headquarter contact. Only in this way can information loops be effectively closed. If there is a weakness in the UNDP clearinghouse function it is in the area of headquarter-to-headquarter communication, that is, in its direct contacts with capitals of donor countries and NGO headquarters. Two examples may be cited to illustrate this problem.

A decision was reached by the UNDP in the spring of 1985 that permitted use of money from its ICARA II Trust Fund to finance joint activities with NGOs. This decision was transmitted to UNDP resident representatives in the field who were instructed to inform NGO representatives of the availability of this money. No systematic effort was made to contact NGO headquarters directly, the assumption perhaps being that they would be duely alerted to this possibility once their field representatives reported back the information rceived from the UNDP resident representatives. But the diligence of NGO field representatives in their reporting function is extremely variable. Thus, only by a long process of word of mouth did many NGO headquarters become aware of this information. A better approach would have been for the UNDP simultaneously to inform NGO headquarters of the availability of these funds, perhaps through ICVA and Interaction, or through a direct and formal announcement. This might have excited a more expeditious NGO response.

Another example illustrates the rather circuitous ways in which some information on donor activities has circulated. Many donors still look to the UNHCR and Geneva as a focal point for ICARA II projects even though the UNDP has formal responsibility for follow-up on infrastructural projects. In one case a major donor informed UNHCR through its Mission in Geneva of its decision to send a mission to Sudan to design a project. This information was formally transmitted by the UNHCR to its representative in Khartoum who informed the local UNDP representative, who in turn informed UNDP headquarters. In this case the information loop was closed by a call from Geneva to New York to confirm the information. However, a more appropriate line of communication would have been for the donor to inform UNDP directly about its plans through its U.N. Mission in New York. But some donor country officials responsible for ICARA II project implementation have been unaware of the role, if not the existence, of the UNDP clearinghouse function, and others are simply not inclined to make use of it.[7] Some donors have yet to attune themselves to working through New York, and lacking a more formal link they are unlikely to do so. For this reason, consideration should be given to the formation of a Liaison Group in New York similar to, but perhaps more informal than, the WHLG which operates in Geneva. Such a focal point would allow UNDP to facilitate communication with the key donor and African missions, and to perform its clearinghouse function more effectively. Alternatively, UNDP might consider beefing up its Geneva presence, since many countries seem irresistably attracted to Geneva when the subject of refugees is involved.

If the UNDP has a central role to play in ICARA II coordination, along with the UNHCR and other U.N. agencies, the host
governments are in an equally crucial position. Without adequate
coordination between the refugee and development ministries
and between the national, regional, and local authorities, it will
be difficult to implement ICARA II projects effectively.

Many donor governments, too, need to more clearly define the
respective authorities and responsibilities of their refugee/human-
itarian and bilateral development agencies. They also should take
steps to ensure that their field representatives are knowledgeable
about the ICARA II process and in contact with appropriate local
officials.

So, too, should NGOs maintain contact both at headquarters
and in the field with governments, the U.N. system and other
NGOs. Indeed the ICVA recommendation that NGOs identify in
each host country a lead agency to facilitate communication with
the donor community and to act as a clearinghouse for information on NGO program opportunities is wholly appropriate.[8]

Because of the decentralized nature of the ICARA II follow-up
process, it is important that all of the relevant actors do their
utmost to announce their intentions and share progress made on
their activities. But formally, at least, the UNDP and host governments have the primary duty to see that adequate coordination is
achieved.

Promotion

The decentralized approach to implementation of ICARA II
projects has meant that promotional efforts must be conducted
almost on a self-help basis. Those asylum countries that have
actively promoted their submissions are most likely to receive
donor attention. Indeed, promotion of ICARA II projects should
be in the interests not only of the host government but of U.N.
agencies and NGOs which may stand to gain as project implementors.

A key aspect of promoting ICARA II projects is to increase
their visibility in the donor community. As has been noted previously, ICARA II has been pushed to the back of the list of
priorities as the international community has responded to the

more pressing needs of the drought emergency.[9] However, a primary tenet of the refugee aid and development dialogue is that refugee aid, and by inference, other forms of emergency assistance, should from the start take into account longer term development factors. The current emergency provides an opportunity for the rhetoric to be put into practice: for emergency drought assistance to anticipate recovery, rehabilitation and long-term development needs. In this sense, the UNGA's 13th Special Session was a clear step in the right direction. Perhaps with the return of rains to many drought-stricken countries, the entire international community will be able to shift into a drought prevention and long term development mode. While several countries, including Angola, Botswana, Ethiopia, and Sudan, continue to be threatened by famine, record harvests in many other areas has demonstrated the resiliency of African agriculture. However, this resilience should not belie the basic vulnerability of food production in Africa. The drought should be seen as a warning of potential future disasters if the international community ignores Africa's tremendous need for agricultural and infrastructural inputs.[10]

In the meantime the ICARA II projects, in many cases, provide excellent opportunities to take concrete actions to address both some of the pressing infrastructural needs and the longer term development horizon. But someone must take the responsibility for reasserting them as priority response to the needs of drought- and refugee-affected areas. The UNDP ICARA II unit has tried to increase ICARA II visibility. The UNHCR has continued to play a very positive role in discussions on refugee aid and development. A few NGOs have also lobbied for ICARA II resources. And recently, donor interest has picked up somewhat.

To ensure that ICARA II and the related themes of refugee aid and development achieve a higher degree of visibility, several steps could be taken:

1. The ICARA II Steering Committee could undertake a trip through Africa to meet with host, donor, U.N. and NGO officials in order to underscore the importance of the ICARA II process and to give it renewed momentum.

2. A joint UNDP-UNHCR sponsored seminar could be held for NGOs to discuss ways that refugee and development aid themes could be disseminated through development education programs so that general public awareness can be raised.

3. The UNHCR and UNDP should each encourage training programs for their field representatives to familiarize them with ICARA II documentation and with the literature on refugee aid and development.
4. The U.N. Institute for Training and Research (UNITAR) could include a modular training component in its courses for development specialists in the U.N. system.
5. ICARA II follow-up should be included on the agendas of the meetings of the governing bodies of the UNHCR, the UNDP and other U.N. specialized agencies to keep donor governments abreast of latest developments and to encourage annual reporting on ICARA II progress. The OAU should continue, as it has in the past, to discuss refugee-related development concerns.
6. The UNHCR and UNDP, as the key operational members of the ICARA II Steering committee, and if necessary the Secretary-General, should try to work closely with groups such as Live Aid and USA for Africa, who have tapped large reservoirs of resources, but lack the skills and expertise to program them effectively. Such groups must be made aware of the longer term development needs of Africa, including the infrastructural needs in refugee- and drought-affected areas, and encouraged to commit a large portion of their revenues to these needs as opposed to only those associated with the emergency.

Ultimately the object of much of this promotional activity will be the donor governments who are in a position to fund concrete programs. Donors cannot be forced to provide resources that do not exist, but in the absence of any promotional efforts on behalf of ICARA II it is unlikely that large amounts of new resources will be forthcoming on an unsolicited basis. Those who stand most to gain from this, that is the host countries themselves, need to take an active promotional stance. In so doing, the OAU could provide a useful forum for them to increase the visibility of the ICARA process.

Evaluation

The long-term success of development programming depends in part on the ability to identify problems and deficiencies with projects and to make adjustments so that future programs more effectively achieve their goals. ICARA II projects will no doubt be subjected to considerable evaluation through the standard bilateral procedures of donor and host countries. It is important that some mechanisms be established to encourage individual donors to share their lessons learned. Otherwise, the decentralized nature of follow-up will limit dissemination of the results of evaluations. Indeed, no provision has been made in the ICARA II Declaration and Programme of Action regarding responsibilities for the conduct or dissemination of project evaluations.

This is where private research organizations and academic institutions could play a useful role. They contributed substantially to the formulation of the basic theories and propositions of the refugee aid and development dialogue, and could provide service by conducting systematic third party assessments of ICARA II projects in the coming years. Several organizations are in a position to sponsor or conduct independent research of this sort, including; the Refugee Policy Group and the Overseas Development Council in Washington, D.C.; the various national refugee councils in Europe; NGO organizations such as ICVA and Interaction; and development-oriented organizations such as the Development Assistance Committee of the OECD. The understanding gained by impartial evaluation and comparative studies of both successful and unsuccessful projects should be of great value to those who design refugee-related development projects in future years. More research also needs to be done on the actual nature of refugee burdens. Some attention has been paid to this since ICARA II, but there is a need for more rigorous and systematic inquiries into the actual impacts of refugees on the environment, housing, education services, health programs and the larger economy of host countries.[11]

Financing for this research could be obtained from a variety of private sources, but some thought should be given over the next few years to the establishment of a Fund (perhaps under the joint auspices of UNHCR and UNDP) to support independent evaluation of this nature.

Beneficiary Participation

The prime beneficiaries of ICARA II projects are, at least in theory, the refugees and host country nationals living in refugee-affected areas. No systematic effort has been or is likely to be taken to ensure that these beneficiaries have a say in the formulation and implementation of projects that are being undertaken by the international community at least nominally on their behalf. In certain individual cases, some effort may have been made to consult the local population, but as a general proposition, they have been ignored. There is no easy way to ensure that the needs of the beneficiary population are being addressed, or to ensure that they have a voice in the process, but the various donors, host countries, NGOs and U.N. agencies that are involved in the process can take steps to increase the beneficial impact of their projects on the intended beneficiaries. These steps would include:

1. Feasibility studies of existing and future projects should examine carefully their relationship to and impact on the beneficiary population.
2. The use of national resources and local building materials for projects should be encouraged.
3. Refugees and nationals with requisite technical expertise should be used wherever possible in project formulation and implementation.
4. Employment and food for work opportunities should be extended to refugees and nationals where appropriate.
5. Projects should contain training components for indigenous personnel (refugees and nationals).
6. Legal and informal host country constraints on refugee participation in these projects should be identified and where possible corrected.
7. Special efforts should be taken to ensure that the needs of refugee and host country women are not ignored.

A TIME FOR SOLUTIONS IN AFRICA AND BEYOND

In recent years, the refugee aid and development dialogue has tended to focus on Africa. Indeed, as early as the 1960s, the OAU was pointing out the connection between refugee and development needs in Africa. ICARA II, as one of the first practical and systematic exercises to do something about refugee-related development burdens further highlighted the particular predicament of Africa. But the principles that have emerged from this process are hardly limited to the African context alone. Indeed, as we have seen, similar principles have been put into action in the World Bank project in Pakistan. Recent NGO discussions on the refugee situation in Central America have touched on similar themes. Indeed, wherever refugees are found in the Third World, the principles of ICARA II are likely to have some bearing. Africa may be the place where the burdens have been most obvious and in greatest need of immediate attention, but it is not the only venue where refugee aid and development principles can be employed usefully.

What sets Africa apart for the time being is that its refugee problem has been aggravated further by the truly desperate economic situation that faces much of the continent. The slogan of ICARA II, 'A Time for Solutions,' which initially referred to the refugee problem, can now be interpreted in a broader and perhaps more prophetic way to include the much larger and graver problems of drought and generalized economic distress. Whether one is dealing with the burden that refugees impose on host countries, or the debilitating impact that drought has had on already enervated economies, there is a common underlying theme: the resource base in Africa is being eroded and the economic infrastructure is grossly inadequate. ICARA II rightly identified these as two of the most critical challenges facing refugee-affected regions, but in truth these are general challenges facing many if not most African countries, whether or not their predicament has been aggravated by the presence of refugees.

When people in the refugee field speak of a need for solutions, they normally refer to the need for political solutions to the problems which spawned refugees in the first place, so that refugees can return safely to their homes. Short of this preferred outcome they refer to the need for settlement of refugees in the countries of first asylum. ICARA II has emphasized that the costs of the latter solution can not be borne alone by already poor countries. It also demonstrated that substantial burdens on the general economic infrastructure of asylum countries are associated with the acceptance of large refugee populations. But the larger problem exists: whether the durable solution is voluntary repatriation or local settlement, the needs of rural Africa in general are sorely in need of attention. Refugees may choose to go home once the political causes of their initial flight have been resolved, but if the land to which they return is barren of trees, if the soil is eroded, if water resources cannot be tapped, if there are no roads to facilitate access to markets, no veterinary attention for their animals, no health or educational services for their families, then it is hard to say that they will be any better off at home than as a refugees in a foreign land. Political solutions are to be sure a prerequisite to the resolution of refugee problems. But solutions to the economic problems of Africa must also be tackled, if the lives of host country nationals, refugees and returnees are to be meaningfully improved. The answer lies in the development of rural Africa.[12] The task is a herculean one, but it can be accomplished if only we recognize not just with our hearts, but with our pocketbooks and heads, that the time for solutions is now.

NOTES

1. See the address of Vice-President George Bush to the U.N. Conference on the African Emergency, 11 March 1985, Geneva Switzerland.
2. Contrast the gloomy picture painted by Lee Lescaze and Steve Mufson, in the *Wall Street Journal,* 15 July 1985, with the more optimistic tone of C. Payne Lucas and Kevin Lowther, 'Is Africa Going Under?' *Washington Post,* 14 July 1985.
3. See A/40/666, Annex I, dec. AHG/Decl.1 (XXI) annex.
4. See UNGA Resolution 39/29 of 3 December 1984 which contains the UN Declaration on the Critical Situation in Africa, and resolution 40/40 of 2 December 1985 which called for the convening the 13th Special Session.
5. For a text of the Final document of the Special Session see, A/RES/S-13/2, Annex.
6. See Appendix 5, and the Report of the Meeting of Experts for more extensive discussions of many of these principles. See also, Clark and Stein, 'A Documentary Note,' for a lucid discussion of the major concepts of the Refugee Aid and Development dialogue.
7. Based on interviews in a number of donor countries I have concluded that this lack of official knowledge in some countries can be attributed mostly to personnel turnover in positions which have been charged with ICARA II follow-up. It suggests that a better job needs to be done in some donor countries to ensure that key information about the ICARA II follow-up process is transmitted to incoming officers by their predecessors. A more

aggressive posture by the UNDP in gathering information from donors might also have salutary effects in this regard.

8. See DePury, 'ICVA Consultants Report,' p. 15.

9. ICARA II's lack of visibility is starkly underscored by the fact that it has gone unmentioned in important international reports. See for instance, *Famine: A Man-made Disaster?* A Report for the Independent Commission on International Humanitarian Issues (ICIHI), (New York: Vintage Books, 1985) which deals extensively with many of the themes enunciated at ICARA II but in which ICARA II, itself, goes unmentioned.

10. See Blaine Harden, 'U.N. Reports Record African Crops,' *Washington Post,* 17 December 1985.

11. Two recent studies have also underscored this need and in modest ways have attempted to come to grips with how to evaluate refugee burdens on host countries. See, Bruce Dick, 'The Impact of Refugees on the Health Status and Services of Host Communities: Compounding Bad with Worse?' *Disasters* 9, 4 (1985): 259–269, and; Lincoln Young, 'A General Assessment of the Environmental Impact of Refugees in Somalia with Attention to the Refugee Agricultural Program,' *Disasters* 9, 2 (1985): 122–133.

12. For an brief but articulate and incisive analysis of how and why rural Africa should be developed, see the ICIHI Report cited supra, note 9.

Appendices

APPENDIX I

ICARA I Resolution
Operative Paragraphs

Resolution 35/42, as recommended by Third Committee as A/35/650 and Corr.1, adopted without vote by the General Assembly on 25 November 1980.

The General Assembly,

. . . .

1. *Notes with profound regret* that the international community has not given sufficient attention to the plight of refugees in Africa;

2. *Requests,* consequently, the international community to contribute substantially to programmes designed to help those refugees;

3. *Approves* the report of the Secretary-General calling for an international conference to mobilize assistance for refugees in Africa, as well as the measures proposed for a concerted programme of information and publicity by the relevant bodies of the United Nations system in support of the conference;

4. *Requests* the Secretary-General, in close co-operation with the Secretary-General of the Organization of African Unity and the United Nations High Commissioner for Refugees, to convene at Geneva on 9 and 10 April 1981, at the ministerial level, an International Conference on Assistance to Refugees in Africa;

5. *Further requests* the Secretary-General in the process of preparing for the Conference, and in close co-operation with the Secretary-General of the Organization of African Unity and the United Nations High Commissioner for Refugees to assist the concerned African countries in identifying priorities and preparing necessary documents and programmes for assistance to African refugees;

6. *Authorizes* the Secretary-General to meet the expenses for organization of the Conference under the regular budget of the United Nations;

7. *Appeals* to the international community, all Member States, the specialized agencies, regional and intergovernmental organizations and non-governmental organizations to provide the utmost support for the Conference with a view to offering maximum financial and material assistance to refugees in Africa;

8. *Further appeals* to the international community to provide all necessary assistance to the countries of asylum to enable them to strengthen their capacity

to provide the necessary facilities and services essential to the care and well-being of the refugees and to assist the countries of origin in the rehabilitation of genuine voluntary returnees;

9. *Urges* the international community to continue to support the annual programmes of the United Nations High Commissioner for Refugees and of other United Nations agencies co-operating with the High Commissioner on behalf of refugees in Africa;

10. *Requests* the High Commissioner, in close co-operation with the Secretary-General of the Organization of African Unity, to keep under constant review the situation of refugees in Africa in order to ensure maximum international assistance on a global basis.

11. *Requests* the Secretary-General to report to the Economic and Social Council at its first regular session of 1981 and to the General Assembly at its thirty-sixth session on the implementation of the present resolution.

APPENDIX II

ICARA II Resolution
Operative Paragraphs

Resolution 37/197, as Recommended by the Third Committee as A/37/L.43, adopted without vote by the General Assembly on 18 December 1982.

The General Assembly,

. . . .

1. *Commends,* the Secretary-General for his reports on the International Conference on Assistance to Refugees in Africa, which were prepared in pursuance of paragraphs 6 and 9 of General Assembly resolution 36/124;

2. *Expresses its appreciation* to all donor countries, the United Nations High Commissioner for Refugees and the international community at large for their continued support and assistance to African refugees, including their efforts to facilitate the process of voluntary repatriation to the countries of origin;

3. *Expresses its concern* that the assistance currently being provided under existing refugee-related programmes falls short of the urgent needs of refugees and returnees in Africa and does not provide sufficient resources to permit the implementation of projects designed to ensure adequate care and relief for the refugees and to expedite the process of rehabilitation and resettlement;

4. *Expresses its appreciation* to the countries of asylum for the great contribution that they are making in alleviating the plight of refugees and urges the international community to give the assistance neccessary to enable those countries to provide essential services and facilities for the refugees;

5. *Requests* the Secretary-General, in close co-operation with the Secretary-General of the Organization of African Unity and the United Nations High Commissioner for Refugees, to convene at Geneva in 1984 a second International Conference on Assistance to Refugees in Africa;

(a) To review thoroughly the results of the Conference held in 1981 as well as the state of progress of the projects submitted to it;

(b) To consider the continuing need for assistance with a view to providing, as necessary, additional assistance to refugees and returnees in Africa for the implementation of programmes for their relief, rehabilitation and resettlement;

(c) To consider the impact imposed on the national economies of the African countries concerned and to provide them with the assistance required to strengthen their social and economic infrastructure so as to enable them to cope with the burden of dealing with large numbers of refugees and returnees;

6. *Also requests* the Secretary-General, in close co-operation with the Secretary-General of the Organization of African Unity and the United Nations High Commissioner for Refugees, to consult with the African countries concerned with regard to their needs for dealing adequately with the problem of refugees and returnees and to submit a report on the situation in each country so as to enable the proposed Conference to have an up-to-date assessment, by priority, of the humanitarian, rehabilitation and resettlement needs of the refugees and returnees, and the assistance required by the countries concerned to strengthen existing services, facilities and infrastructure and, for that purpose, to reallocate existing resources.

7. *Calls upon* the competent specialized agencies and organizations of the United Nations system, including the development-oriented organizations, to provide all necessary co-operation and support to the Secretary-General in respect of the report called for in paragraph 6 above, to be prepared for the Conference to be held in 1984;

8. *Requests* the Secretary-General to ensure that adequate financial and budgetary arrangements are made to cover the expenses involved in the preparation of the report, as well as those for the organization of the Conference in 1984;

9. *Appeals* to the international community, all Member States, the specialized agencies and regional, intergovernmental and non-governmental organizations to provide the utmost support for the Conference with a view to offering maximum financial and material assistance to refugees and returnees in Africa;

10. *Invites* the executive bodies of the specialized agencies and intergovernmental and non-governmental organizations to bring the present resolution to the attention of their members and to consider, within their respective spheres of competence, various ways and means subtantially to increase assistance to African refugees and returnees;

11. *Stresses* that any additional assistance provided for refugee-related projects should not be at the expense of the development needs of the countries concerned;

12. *Requests* the Secretary-General to report to the General Assembly at its thirty-eighth session on the implementation of the present resolution.

APPENDIX III

Guidelines for Preparation of ICARA II Submissions

Guidelines for Country Submissions on the Impact of Refugee Problems on National Economies and Possible Development Assistance Required to Alleviate These Problems.

1. In briefing representatives of the donor community and of the affected African countries at meetings held in New York on 23 February 1983, on preparations for ICARA II, the Secretary-General emphasized that requests for assistance to strengthen existing services, facilities and infrastructure should be directly related to refugee situations. Moreover, requests should be kept within reasonable bounds and be supported by detailed project proposals. The Secretary-General also mentioned that the resources might not be readily available on a scale commensurate with the needs of the refugee situations. It was, therefore, esssential that projects and programmes submitted should be convincing enough to obtain the attention and support of the donor community.

2. A major objective of ICARA II will be to acquaint the international community with the nature and extent of the burden borne by African countries owing to the presence of large numbers of refugees, and to seek ways and means of mobilizing additional assistance to help them cope with this burden.

3. The country submission should provide a careful review and assessment by the Government concerned of the burden caused by the refugee situation and of the on-going and additional requirements necessary to deal with these problems in the short, medium and long term . . .

4. Governments may be assisted in the preparation of their submission by the Resident Representative of the United Nations Development Programme and by the local representative of the United Nations High Commissioner for Refugees. The UNDP Resident Representative will also be able to co-ordinate inputs from other relevant United Nations agencies and organizations. Before finalizing their submissions, Governments might also find it useful to exchange views with local donor Governments and voluntary representatives. Submissions should be completed by 30 June 1983 and should by that time be available in the Office of the UNDP Resident Representative for consideration by the technical mission which will consult with the government concerned prior to its finalization. The technical team will visit the affected African countries between July and October 1983.

5. Governments, when preparing submissions, should bear in mind that the technical team will already have available relevant background information on the overall economic situation of each country. The team will also have information from existing reports on the size and nature of the refugee problem in each country seeking additional assisstance, and on the size and nature of past relief, rehabilitation, local settlement or repatriation efforts. During its visit, the team may seek clarification or additional information regarding some of these matters. In addition, the team will have submissions on the humanitarian programmes, now being prepared by UNHCR in consultation with the Governments concerned.

6. In view of the availability of the above information, the contents of the country submission should focus primarily on the following:

I.   Government policy in regard to refugees (including where relevant, efforts to reach a durable long-term solution).
II. Impact of refugees on the national economy.
III. Overall plans designed to deal with the refugee situation and particularly development projects (if any) for consideration at ICARA II.

7. It is understood that African countries with relatively small refugee burdens, or where integration or other solutions are already well advanced, may not have specific additional proposals for projects relevant to the Conference. In such cases only a general statement on the economic impact is required.

I. GOVERNMENT POLICY IN REGARD TO REFUGEES

8. It would be useful to have available in the documentation for ICARA II a clear statement of the Government's policy regarding refugees or returnees, and particularly, where relevant, prospects for as well as obstacles to a lasting solution.

II. IMPACT OF REFUGEES ON THE NATIONAL ECONOMY

9. Many countries in Africa affected by refugee problems fall within the group of countries generally referred to as least developed. Others are only marginally better off. The carrying of additional financial and other material burdens owing to the presence of substantial numbers of refugees within their territories has in many cases, strained their already meagre resources and contributed to a further weakening of their economies. It would be helpful if each country so affected could provide as much detailed, objective and quantitative data as possible to estimate or measure this burden. It is recognized that much of this information may be difficult to quantify with any precision in the limited time available. However, every effort should be made in this regard to ensure an effective submission for ICARA II.

10. An attempt should be made to provide a reasonable assessment of the actual impact that the presence of refugees is continuing to have on the local and

national economy. Data should include information on direct and indirect on-going assistance (financial, personnel, or in-kind) provided by the host Government to refugees. The technical team will examine submissions made by each Government and assist in their elaboration, with the aim of ensuring reasonable comparability in the methods used for measuring the burden in different countries.

11. While it is appreciated that such information may not be readily available, Governments are requested to provide as much as possible in terms of figures, or by a brief description of the present costs related to the impact of refugees or returnees. It should cover such areas as:

(a) Infrastructural development

The increment in capital expenditures for infrastructural development in specified areas to cater for additional needs created by the presence of refugees. Those could include expenditure in the following categories:

(i) Education, primary, secondary or university;
(ii) Hospitals, clinics and health centres;
(iii) Transportation and communication facilities;
(iv) Water and other utilities;
(v) Environmental situation.

(b) Food and basic needs

Direct assistance in the form of food being supplied in kind by the host Government, as well as similar information in respect of clothing, shelter, medicines and other health and sanitary supplies.

(c) Budgetary support

Direct contributions by the host Government in the form of annual budgetary allocations for:

(i) General upkeep of refugees;
(ii) Capital development in refuge areas; and
(iii) Maintenance of infrastructure in refugee camps and other areas predominantly occupied by refugees.

(d) Administrative and technical support

Information on numbers and categories of administrative and technical personnel of the host Government assigned exclusively to refugee activities and borne by the national budget.

180

(e) Use of agricultural and industrial resources

Allocation of land for agricultural, housing and other purposes.

(f) Employment

A brief description of employment and income-earning opportunities for refugees inside or outside the refugee areas. If relevant assess the impact of such employment on the general labour situation of the country.

(g) Balance of payments

Estimates of the impact of refugees on the country's balance of payments, including information on:
(i)   The allocation of foreign exchange resources by the Government for the import of food, medicines, equipment, etc., for use by refugees;
(ii) The value of foreign products and supplies in kind or as cash grants, provided by donor agencies;
(iii) The value of local supplies purchased with foreign assistance;
(iv) External loans or credits for support of refugee-related activities.

(h) Cost of living

An indication of the adverse impact, where pertinent, on the cost of living of the indigenous population in refugee settlement areas, e.g., rents, food, utilities, etc.

(i) General

An assessment of the impact of refugees in terms of the burdens (costs) which they impose and the contributions (benefits) that refugee populations make to the GDP and to various areas of the national economy of the host country. Indicate the extent to which the National Development Plan has taken into account the refugee problem. Where relevant, indicate how planned or on-going development projects within the country may alleviate the refugee situation.

III. DEVELOPMENT PROJECTS FOR CONSIDERATION AT ICARA II

12. As UNHCR will consult directly with the Governments concerned on requests for additional humanitarian assistance, projects falling under the above heading should be confined to refugee-related projects which are developmental in nature. The projects should be presented on a priority basis within the framework of the National Development Plan. The list should emphasize *additional* development projects, which can be directly justified as ameliorating the problems posed by the presence of refugees or facilitating long-term solutions.

13. This priority list of additional development projects requiring funding for consideration by ICARA II should consist of a one-page summary for each project. These summaries should include, particularly for larger projects, reference to sources for more detailed information, such as full project documents or feasibility studies. The description of each should be uniform and should indicate:

(a) The type and number of refugees involved;
(b) The costs for each project, and where appropriate, showing direct foreign exchange costs, and the Government's own contributions, where relevant;
(c) Whether the project is entirely new, or if not, what efforts towards funding of the project were made in the past, and any other obstacles in proceeding with the project;
(d) The time-frame of the project;
(e) The future financing consequences for each project (e.g. rquirements for maintenance or upkeep after completion, and the extent to which these can be met from local budgetary resources);
(f) A clear justification for each project in terms of its relevance to refugees.

14. Every effort should be made to comply with donor agency project formulation requirements (such as those of UNDP and the World Bank) to ensure more effective projects and to attract funding.

15. It is essential for the success of the Conference that Governments give a clear indication of priorities with respect to funding of their proposed development projects on behalf of refugees.

ICARA II Final Declaration
and Program of Action

Declaration and Programme of Action of the Second International Conference on Assistance to Refugees in Africa.

I. DECLARATION

A. Global Responsibility

1. The task of caring for refugees and finding solutions to their problems is a matter of international concern in keeping with the Charter of the United Nations and other international instruments, in particular the 1951 United Nations Convention relating to the Status of Refugees and its 1967 Protocol. The Conference recognizes that the condition of refugees is a global responsibility of the international community and emphasizes the need for equitable burden-sharing by all its members, taking into consideration particularily the case of the least developed countries.

B. Continental responsibility

2. In dealing with the refugee situation in Africa, special account must be taken of the regional situation and of the regionally relevant legal instruments, such as the Charter of the Organizations of African Unity (OAU), conventions as well as principles mentioned in resolutions adopted under the auspices of OAU.

C. 1969 OAU Convention

3. The 1969 OAU Convention Governing the Specific Aspects of Refugee Problems in Africa constitutes a basic instrument for the plight of refugees in that continent; according to article VIII, paragraph 2, the OAU Convention shall be the effective regional complement in Africa of the 1951 United Nations Convention on the Status of Refugees. Accession to the OAU Convention by African States that have not yet done so, respect for the principles contained

therein and the most rigorous care in their daily implementation must remain the foundation for protecting and assisting refugees in Africa. The principle enshrined in the 1969 Convention that 'the granting of asylum is a peaceful and humanitarian act and shall not be regarded as an unfriendly act by any Member State' must continue to guide the approach of States to the refugee problem in Africa.

D. Arusha Conference

4. The recommendations of the 1979 Arusha Conference on the Situation of Refugees in Africa, endorsed by the OAU Council of Ministers through its resolution CM /Res.727 (XXXIII) and reaffirmed by the General Assembly of the United Nations in its resolutions 34/61 of 29 November 1979 and 35/41 A of 25 November 1980, remain fundamental for action on behalf of refugees in Africa. The recommendations deal with the causes for asylum seeking in Africa and the situation of rural and urban refugees, their employment, education and training, and arrangements for refugee counselling services.

5. The Arusha Conference also adopted a number of recommendations relating to the legal situation of refugees, notably as regards asylum, the definition of the refugee concept and the determination of refugee status, illegal entry and expulsion, rights and obligations of refugees and voluntary repatriation. The standards defined in these recommendations, together with those figuring in the 1969 OAU Convention, represent an important component for the protection of and assistance to refugees in the African continent. The Organization of African Unity and the Office of the United Nations High Commissioner for Refugees (UNHCR) are urged, in accordance with a decision of that Conference, to continue monitoring the implementation of the relevant recommendations and report thereon through the appropriate channels.

E. Meeting between the OAU secretariat and voluntary agencies

6. The 92 recommendations adopted in March 1983 at the meeting between the OAU secretariat and voluntary agencies dealt with the following issues: Second International Conference on Assistance to Refugees in Africa, protection, voluntary repatriation, awareness-building and public information, co-operation in refugee assistance at the national, regional and international levels, root causes of refugee situations, education, counselling, settlement and resettlement, and role of voluntary agencies during emergencies, which should constitute a realistic approach to the refugee problem in Africa.

F. OAU Charter on Human and People's Rights

7. Respect for human and people's rights and benefit from economic and social progress and development in conformity with Article 55 of the Charter of the United Nations must be a corner-stone in the protection of and assistance to refugees. The Conference takes full note of the adoption by the OAU Heads of

State and Government of the Charter on Human and People's Rights, the entry into force of which will constitute a positive contribution in reducing the number of refugees in Africa.

G. Approaches to solutions

8. International co-operation to avert new flows of refugees must be strengthened. Everything possible must be done to prevent the causes of refugee flows and to reduce and resolve the problem of refugees in Africa. States must refrain from taking measures that would create or aggravate refugee problems. Essential conditions should be established to facilitate the voluntary repatriation of refugees, which has been recognized as the best means of promoting permanent and durable solutions. This could be done by the promulgation of amnesty laws and respect for the principle of *non-refoulement*. Where voluntary return is not immediately feasible or possible, conditions should be created within the country of asylum for a temporary settlement or the integration of refugees into the community and their full participation in its social and economic life. For solutions to last, assistance to refugees and returnees must aim at their participation, productivity and durable self-reliance; it should be development-oriented as soon as possible and, in least developed countries, it should take into account the needs of the local people as well.

II. PROGRAMME OF ACTION

A. Voluntary Repatriation

1. Voluntary repatriation remains, when conditions allow, the ideal solution to a refugee problem. Governments are responsible for creating the necessary legal and practical conditions conducive to the return of refugees. The Office of the United Nations High Commissioner for Refugees (UNHCR) is, by its mandate, required to facilitate the return of refugees and safeguard its voluntary nature; it should take all measures deemed appropriate, tripartite commissions composed of representatives of the country of origin, the country of asylum and UNHCR should be established; in this process, care must be taken to respect the voluntary nature of the repatriation process and the entirely non-political character of the work of UNHCR.

2. For the ultimate aim of successful reintegration of returnees into their society, rehabilitation assistance will often be required well beyond the initial period during which UNHCR can provide it. In such cases, the United Nations Development Programme (UNDP) and other relevant development organizations and non-governmental organizations should be involved as soon as possible in the planning and implementation of further rehabilitation assistance which may benefit not only returnees but also their compatriots in the areas concerned.

B. Local settlement

3. Where voluntary repatriation is not immediately feasible or possible, conditions should be created within the country of asylum so that the refugees can temporarily settle or integrate into the community, i.e., participate on an equal footing in its social and economic life and contribute to its development. For this purpose, settlement programmes should be development-oriented and, wherever possible, be linked to existing or planned economic and social development schemes for the area or region.

4. When large numbers of refugees need land or other work opportunities, there is a need for development-oriented projects which would generate work opportunities and – where local integration of the refugees is feasible – long-term livelihoods for refugees and local people in a comparable situation, through activities which create assets of a continuing economic value with a good rate of return, so that they contribute to the overall development of the area.

C. Infrastructural assistance

5. As a result of the adverse impact on the national economies of the African countries concerned, most of which belong to the group of the least developed countries, there is need to provide these countries with the required assistance to strengthen their social and economic infrastructure so as to enable them to cope with the burden of dealing with large numbers of refugees and returnees. This assistance, to achieve the desired objective, should be aditional to, and not at the expense of, concerned countries' other development programmes.

D. The process

6. The international community, through the Second International Conference on Assistance to Refugees in Africa, will endeavour to provide assistance at three levels:

(a) The necessary relief and care and maintenance must be provided to refugees in the face of an emergency; it must be adjusted to the immediate needs of refugees, be directly linked to those needs and be commensurate with reliable estimates of their numbers.

(b) Long-term solutions, through voluntary repatriation of refugees or their settlement in countries of asylum, must be continued and, as necessary, expanded; additional resources should be made available for expanded durable solutions efforts.

(c) Technical and capital assistance to countries that offer asylum to refugees and to countries that welcome back returnees should be recognized as an important new element of international assistance; such assistance should be additional to ongoing development programmes. The Conference expresses the hope that the commitments as undertaken at the Conference will be fulfilled as soon as possible.

E. Structures for assistance to refugees, including returnees, and for co-ordination of such aid and development assistance

7. The complementarity between refugee-related aid and development assistance should be reflected in the structures addressing these issues.

8. In aid to refugees, both for relief, care and maintenance and towards durable solutions through local settlement and voluntary repatriation, UNHCR should remain the focal point and should closely co-operate with other relevant bodies within and outside the United Nations system.

9. Closer co-ordination between refugee and returnee services and development services within the administrative framework of countries receiving refugees or returnees would contribute to the development-orientation of refugee projects from the earliest possible stage.

10. Likewise, closer co-operation of development services in the financial donor countries would be conducive to addressing the refugee problem in its development context.

11. Governing councils of development agencies should seriously consider the refugee and returnee element in their programme planning with a view to alleviating the plight of refugees and returnees. Among such agencies UNDP, in view of its central co-ordinating role within the United Nations system for development and its close linkages with donor communities, could be asked to take as soon as possible a leading part in the co-ordination, implementation and monitoring of refugee-related infrastructural projects of a developmental nature in close association with its partners and other donors; the expertise of non-governmental organizations, in the assessment, planning and execution of projects should also be utilized.

F. Follow-up of the Second International Conference on Assistance to Refugees in Africa

12. The Second International Conference on Assistance to Refugees in Africa is another important step of a long-term process on the road towards lasting solutions to the problems of refugees and returnees in Africa. Further fact-finding missions, accurate data collection activities and feasibility studies may be necessary in many cases in furthering this process.

13. The Secretary-General of the United Nations, in consultation and close co-operation with the Organization of African Unity, is requested to monitor through the existing channels the follow-up of the Conference and to recommend the appropriate action needed for this purpose.

14. Governments are requested to keep the Secretary-General of the United Nations informed of any action taken or being taken relating to the projects submitted to the Conference, through UNHCR in the case of projects submitted or which may be submitted in response to paragraph 5 (b) of General Assembly resolution 37/197 and through the office of the Secretary-General and/or UNDP in the case of projects submitted in response to paragraph 5 (c) of that resolution.

15. The Secretary-General is requested to submit to the General Assembly at its thirty-ninth session a first report on the results of the Conference as well as action taken or planned to follow up on the process initiated at the Conference.

APPENDIX V

Refugee Aid and Development, Principles for Action in Developing Countries*

Durable solutions

(a) Refugee problems demand durable solutions. A genuinely durable solution means integration of the refugees into a society, either re-integration in the country of origin, after voluntary repatriation, or integration in the country of asylum or country of resettlement.

(b) Resettlement in third countries, which is a necessary solution in certain circumstances, is the least desirable and most costly solution, so that for refugees in most countries a durable solution should be sought through repatriation to their country of origin, which is the best option wherever it is voluntarily accepted by the refugees, or through settlement in the country of asylum.

(c) In either case, the solution will be lasting only if it allows the refugees or returnees to support themselves and participate in the social and economic life of the community on an equal footing with the surrounding population, and this should therefore be the ultimate aim of assistance to refugees.

Temporary measures pending a durable solution

(d) Where voluntary return is not immediately feasible, conditions should be created in the country of asylum for temporary settlement of the refugees and their participation in the social and economic life of the community, so that they can contribute to its development. For the refugees it is essential to free themselves from dependence on relief, and reach a situation where they can take care of themselves, as soon as possible.

(e) From the outset, therefore, their productivity should be encouraged through self-help activities, engagement in food or other agricultural production, participation in local works to improve economic and social infrastructure, or skills-training projects.

(f) In low-income areas, the needs of the local people should also be taken into account, in such areas developmental initiatives may therefore be needed which would permit both refugees and local people to engage in economically pro-

* A/AC.96/645 Annex I.

ductive activities to ensure them a decent livelihood. Suh initiatives do not necessarily imply a commitment to one or another longer-term solution.

Settlement in country of asylum

(g) Developmental initiatives will be necessary in areas where significant numbers of refugees (in comparison with the local population) need income-earning opportunities, in these areas development-oriented projects are required that would generate work opportunities and – where local integration of the refugees is feasible – long-term livelihoods for refugees and local people in a comparable situation, through activities which create assets of a continuing economic value with a good rate of return, so that they contribute to the overall development of the area.

(h) While such projects should be linked, wherever possible, to existing or planned development schemes for the area, and should always be planned in the context of the host country's development plans, they should be additional to, and not at the expense of, the country's ongoing development programmes.

Roles of UNHCR and other bodies

(i) UNHCR, while being the focal point for durable solutions, should not assume the role of a development agency, and where developmental initiatives are needed, the High Commissioner's role should be essentially that of a catalyst and coordinator, he should initiate suitable projects, promote their development by a competent organization and the host government, and then promote their financing and their implementation and monitor the results for the refugees.

(j) Under its normal programmes UNHCR should continue, in close cooperation with other organizations of the UN system and NGOs, to seek durable solutions through projects planned specifically for the refugees, even though local people also may eventually benefit from some of them.

(k) Where the need is for developmental projects conceived from the outset for both refugees and local people with similar needs in a given area, UNHCR should, in consultation with the host government, invite a developmental organization – international, national or non-governmental – to provide its services for the formulation, appraisal, negotiation and supervision of appropriate projects. They would normally be implemented by, or under the responsibility of, the host government, where necessary with the assistance of suitable executing organizations which might be non-governmental; such organizations should be brought in as early as possible. UNHCR could provide its good offices for the financing of such projects, and would need to follow them closely to ensure that the refugees benefit as planned.

(l) Development projects aimed essentially at improving a host country's economic or social infrastructure, which help it cope with the presence of refugees but do not directly benefit significant numbers of refugees, should be handled, as a rule, by UNDP and/or other developmental organizations including NGOs; as those under (k) above, such projects should normally be additional to, and not at the expense of, the country's other development programmes. Where the projects can be broadened in scope to provide durable income-earning opportunities for refugees, UNHCR could contribute to their financing in proportion to the number of refugees among the beneficiaries.

(m) In the case of large-scale voluntary repatriation to a low-income country, an international commitment to help is needed to achieve successful re-integration, and this may need to include, beyond UNHCR's programmes, developmental investments for the benefit of the returnees that would also benefit their compatriots in the areas concerned. In such cases, UNDP and/or other relevant developmental organizations and NGOs should be involved as soon as possible in the planning of further appropriate rehabilitation assistance.

(n)In all phases of a refugee problem it is important that the beneficiaries of projects be involved in their planning, management and implementation as much as possible.

Co-ordination measures

(o) Governing bodies of development agencies should consider the presence of substantial numbers of refugees or returnees as one of the relevant elements in their programme planning.

(p) The complementarity between refugee aid and development assistance should be reflected in the structures and coordination procedures for addressing these issues at the national level – in both the host countries and the assisting countries – as well as within and between the international organizations concerned.

(q) Proper coordination of refugee-related development projects with other development projects, in the context of the host country's development strategy, should take place on a country basis through existing consultative mechanisms such as Consultative Group or Consortium meetings or Round Table conferences; where a country has received substantial numbers of refugees so that their presence affects its development, refugee-related development assistance should be reviewed as a regular part of these consultative processes.

Guidelines for UNHCR/UNDP Cooperation with Regard to Development Activities Affecting Refugees

The following provisions will guide the enhancement of UNHCR/UNDP co-operation in the areas of mutual interest identified in these provisions. They complement existing arrangements for co-operation between both organizations.

1. The initiative for UNDP involvement in a project related to or involving refugees must come from UNHCR and the recipient government.

2. Where projects necessary to enable refugees to support themselves or to integrate into the local community need to go beyond the scope of UNHCR programmes, i.e. need to benefit also substantial numbers of local people and contribute to the development of the area, it may be appropriate for UNDP to be involved, at the request of UNHCR and the government concerned, in the formulation and implementation of such projects.

3. There is nothing to preclude a government from including in its IPF-funded programme a project or project elements which are refugee-related in the sense that although these activities are of a primarily developmental nature, refugees may be included among its beneficiaries. In such cases in consultation with UNHCR on issues which affect refugees, normal UNDP programming and implementation procedures and arrangements would apply, and UNDP Resident Representatives should then urge governments to take explicit account of the refugee situations and their development aspects in country programming and review exercises. Similarly, the Administrator, at the request of the Government(s) concerned, may use other funds under his authority, as appropriate.

4. For projects funded jointly from UNDP resources and through UNHCR and/or third parties, the mechanism for UNDP cost-sharing may be utilized.

5. In cases where full funding is to be provided through UNHCR and/or third parties, the UNDP trust fund mechanism would apply.

6. When required, UNDP and UNHCR would collaborate in seeking appropriate funding from third parties.

7. Normal UNDP procedures and arrangements should be followed for the programming and timely implementation (including project identification, preparation, appraisal, implementation, monitoring and evaluation) of projects covered under paragraphs 4 and 5 above. Action in this context should lead to the

earliest possible implementation of the project(s) concerned. As these projects are UNDP-UNHCR joint ventures, the closest possible consultations should be held between the two organizations, in particular in the formulation, appraisal and evaluation stages of the project. Support costs to UNDP and executing agencies would be paid in accordance with arrangements applicable to the method of financing involved and would be met from such financing sources.

8. In addition to these types of co-operation, UNDP may provide upon request specified management and/or technical services to UNHCR or a third party in the formulation, execution or evaluation of a project. In such cases, UNDP will charge a fee calculated to cover fully UNDP's costs. Where appropriate, UNDP would consult with specialized agencies in the provision of such services.

9. Under currently applicable UNDP Governing Council decisions, UNDP would make appropriate charges to other UN executing agencies for any services which UNDP field offices might provide to such agencies in connection with the execution of non-UNDP trust fund activities negotiated directly by the agency with donors. When services by OPE are involved, the combined UNDP and OPE support costs will not exceed the authorized standard support costs applicable to UN system executing agencies.

10. The Government should be requested to determine, from the beginning of any UNDP-UNHCR activity, which ministry or body at the central government level will act as the principal co-ordinating authority during the implementation of such activity.

11. While informal consultations and proposals at the field level between UNDP Resident Representatives and UNHCR Representatives are encouraged, formal arrangements for joint endeavors will be decided upon at the Headquarters level. Both Headquarters, as well as the respective field offices involved, will oversee the remaining action to be taken.

12. As soon as it becomes clear in a given refugee situation that significant developmental activities affecting both refugees and nationals of the host country will be required, UNDP should be informed and may be involved where appropriate as per paragraphs 1 and 2 above.

Selected Bibliography

WORKS OF IMPORTANCE TO REFUGEE AID AND DEVELOPMENT

Barber, Martin. 'Voluntary Agency Perspectives on Refugee Aid and Development'. Paper presented at the ICVA General Conference Meetings. Dakar, Senegal. May 1985.

Berar-Awad, Azita, ed. *Towards Self-Reliance: A Programme of Action for Refugees in Eastern and Central Sudan.* [A Joint UNHCR/ILO Project.] Geneva: International Labour Organisation, 1984.

Betts, T.F. (edited by Shelly Pitterman), 'Evolution and Promotion of the Integrated Rural Development Approach to Refugee Policy in Africa', Africa today, 31, 1 (1984): 7–24.

Birido, Omer. 'International Conference on Assistance to Refugees in Africa (ICARA) and its Aftermath'. Paper presented to the Khartoum Refugee Seminar. September 1982.

British Refugee Council. 'Africa's Refugee Crisis: New Directions for Assistance, Aid and Development'. June 1984.

Chambers, Robert. 'Hidden Losers The Impact of Rural Refugees and Refugee Programs on Poorer Hosts', *International Migration Review* (hereinafter *IMR*), Special Issue edited by Dennis Gallagher on Refugees: Issues and Directions, 20 (Summer 1986): 245–263.

Chambers, Robert. 'Rural refugees in Africa: Past Experience, Future Pointers', *Disasters* 6 (1982): 21–30.

Chambers, Robert. 'Rural Refugees in Africa: What the Eye Does Not See'. *Disasters* 3 (1979): 381–392.

Christensen, Hanne. *Survival Strategies for and by Camp Refugees.* U.N. Research Institute for Social Development. Report No. 82.3. Geneva, Switzerland, 1982.

Christensen, Hanne. *Sustaining Afghan Refugees in Pakistan: Report on the Food Situation and Related Social Aspects.* Geneva: U.N. Research Institute for Social Development, 1983.

Clark, D. Lance and Stein, Barry. 'The Relationship Between ICARA II and Refugee Aid and Development'. *Migration Today* 13, 1 (1985): 33–38.

Cuny, Frederick. *Disasters and Development.* Oxford: Oxford University Press: 1983.

194

de Cuellar, Javier Perez. 'Secretary-General's Statement to Meeting of Donor Countries Concerning 1984 Conference on Refugees in Africa'. Economic Commission for Africa, Information Service. Press Release No. 2725. 25 February 1983.

DePury, David. 'Report to ICVA on ICARA II Follow-up'. Paper delivered at the ICVA General Conference Meetings, Dakar, Senegal, May 1985.

Dewey, A.E. 'Refugee Aid and Development'. U.S. Statement to the Informal UNHCR Executive Committee. Geneva: January, 1984.

Dick, Bruce. 'The Impact of Refugees on the Health Status and Services of Host Communities: Compounding Bad With Worse?' *Disasters* 9, 4 (1985): 259–269.

Eriksson, L.G., *et al.*, eds. *An Analyzing Account of the Conference on the African Refugee Problem: Arusha, May 1979*. Uppsala, Sweden: Scandinavian Institute of African Studies (SIAS), 1981.

European Communities. *Draft Report on Assistance to Refugees in Developing Countries*. Committee on Development and Cooperation for the European Parliament, 1983.

Finley, Terence. 'The Permanent Settlement of African Refugees'. *IMR* 13 (1975): 92–105.

Gallagher, Dennis and Stein, Barry. 'ICARA II: Burden Sharing and Durable Solutions'. Washington, D.C.: Refugee Policy Group. 1984.

Goodwillie, Susan. 'Refugees in the Developing World: A Challenge to the International Community'. Prepared for the UNHCR sponsored Meeting of Experts on Refugee Aid and Development. Mont Pelerin, Switzerland. August 1983.

Gorman, Robert F. 'Beyond ICARA II: Implementing Refugee-Related Development Assistance', *IMR* 20 Special Issue on Refugees (Summer 1986): 283–298.

Hansen, Art. 'Refugee Dynamics: Angolans in Zambia 1966 to 1972'. *IMR* 15, 1–2 (Spring-Summer): 175–194.

Harrell-Bond, Barbara, *Imposing Aid: Emergency Assistance to Refugees* (Oxford: Oxford University Press, 1985).

Hartling, Poul. 'Refugee Aid and Development: Genesis and Testing of a Strategy'. *World Refugee Survey, 1984*. New York: U.S. Committee for Refugees (1984): 16–19.

'ICARA II: Development Efforts Needed to Aid 4 Million Refugees in Africa'. *U.N. Chronicle* 21, 6 (1984): 3–11.

International Catholic Migration Committee. 'Re: "Refugee Aid and Development" One Agency's Response'. *Migration News* (1984, no. 1): 25–26.

International Council of Voluntary Agencies. *Timely Solutions: Voluntary Agencies and African Refugees*. Geneva, 1984.

International Conference on Assistance to Refugees in Africa. *Refugees in Africa: A Country by Country Survey*. Geneva: UNHCR.

International Labour Organisation. *Tradition and Dynamism among Afghan Refugees: A Report on Income-Generating Activities for Afghan Refugees in Pakistan*. [A joint UNHCR/ILO Project.] Geneva: ILO, 1983.

Jacobs, Scott and Paar, Kathy. 'An Assessment of the Economic Integration of Urban Refugees in Port Sudan, Gedaref and Kassala'. Khartoum, Sudan: Office of Refugee Affairs, U.S. Embassy, 1983.

Karadawi, Ahmed. 'Constraints on Assistance to Refugees: Some Observations from Sudan'. *World Development* 11 (1983): 537–547.

Keely, Charles. *Global Refugee Policy: The Case for a Development-Oriented Strategy.* Washington, D.C.: The Population Council, 1981.

Keller, Stephen L. *Uprooting and Social Change: The Role of Refugees in Development.* Delhi: Manohar Book Service, 1975 (2nd edition, 1984).

Khan, Sadruddin Aga. *Study on Human Rights and Massive Exoduses.* United Nations Economic and Social Council. E/CN.4/1503. Commission on Human Rights. December 1981.

Neldner, Brian. 'Settlement of Rural Refugees in Africa'. *Disasters* 3 (1979): 393–402.

Refugee Policy Group. 'ICARA II: Future Directions for Assistance to Refugees in Africa'. Washington, D.C.: 1984.

Refugee Studies Program. Oxford Symposium Report. 'Assistance to Refugees: Alternative Viewpoints'. March 1984.

Scudder, Thayer. 'From Relief to Development: Some Comments on Refugee and Other Settlement in Somalia'. Paper prepared for U.S. AID. June, 1981.

Scudder, Thayer and Colson, Elizabeth. 'From Welfare to Development: A Conceptual Framework for the Analysis of Dislocated People'. In *Involuntary Migration and Resettlement.* edited by Art Hansen and Anthony Oliver Smith. Boulder, CO: Westview Press, 1982.

Smyser, William R. Interview by Tony Hodges. *Africa Report* 29, 1 (January-February 1984): 4–10.

Smythe, Mabel M. 'African Refugees: Their Impact on Economic Development in Countries of Asylum'. *Issue: A Journal of Africanist Opinion* 12, 1–2 (Spring-Summer, 1982): 7–9.

Stein, Barry. 'Refugees and Economic Activities in Africa'. Paper presented at the Khartoum Seminar on Refugees. Khartoum, Sudan. September, 1982.

Sudan. National Committee for Aid to Refugees. *Report: International Conference on Refugees in Sudan.* June, 1980.

Trappe, P. *Social Change and Development Institutions in a Refugee Population.* Geneva: U.N. Research Institute for Social Development, 1971.

UNHCR *Establishment of a UNHCR Fund for Durable Solutions.* A/AC.96/569. Executive Committee, Thirtieth sess., August, 1979.

UNHCR. *Working Group on the UNHCR Fund for Durable Solutions.* A/AC.96/582. Executive Committee. Thirty-first sess. August, 1980.

UNHCR. *Managing Rural Settlements for Refugees in Africa.* Geneva, 1981.

UNHCR. *ICARA: The Refugee Situation in Africa: Assistance Measures Proposed.* A/CONF.106/1. Geneva, 1981.

UNHCR. ICARA. *Refugees in Africa: A Country by Country Survey.* Geneva 1981.

UNHCR. 'The Refugee Problem in a Development Context'. Prepared for OECD, Geneva, 1981.

UNHCR. *Report of the Meeting of Experts on Refugee Aid and Development.* Mount Pelerin, Switzerland. August, 1983.

UNHCR. 'Refugees in Africa: NGOs, ICARA II and Beyond'. In *Timely Solutions: Voluntary Agencies and African Refugees.* Geneva: ICVA, 1984.

UNCHR. *Refugee Aid and Development.* A/AC.96/SR375. October 1984.

UNHCR. *ICARA II: From the Press.* Geneva, 1984.

UNHCR. *Follow-up of ICARA II: Status Report as of 15 April 1985.* Memo. Regional Bureau for Africa to UNHCR Staff Members at Headquarters and in the Field. May 1985.

World Bank. *Staff Appraisal Report: Pakistan: Income Generating Project for Refugee Areas.* Washington, D.C. 1983.

Young, Lincoln. 'A General Assessment of the Environmental Impact of Refugees in Somalia with Attention to the Refugee Agricultural Program', *Disasters* 9, 2 (1985): 122–133.

WORKS ON THE GENERAL AFRICAN REFUGEE SITUATION

Adepoju, Aderanti. 'The Dimension of the Refugee Problem in Africa'. *African Affairs* 81 (1982): 21–35.

Brooks, H.C., and El-Ayouty, Yassin, eds. *Refugees South of the Sahara.* Westport, Ct: Negro Universities Press, 1970.

Crisp, Jeff. 'Voluntary Repatriation Programmes for African Refugees: A Critical Examination'. *Refugee Issues* 1, 2 (1984).

Davis, Morris, ed. *Civil Wars and the Politics of International Relief.* New York: Praeger, 1975.

Finland. *Mechanization of Agriculture in the Refugee Settlement Areas of the Eastern Sudan: A Summary of the Joint Finnish-Sudanese Project Review Mission.* Helsinki: Finnida, December 1984.

Food and Agricultural Organization (FAO). 'Special Report on Food Supply Situation in African Countries Affected By Food and Agricultural Emergencies in 1984/1985'. Rome, December 1984.

Franke, Richard W. and Chasin, Barbara H. *Seeds of Famine: Ecological Destruction and the Development Dilemma in the West African Sahel.* Montclair, N.J.: Allanheld Osmun, 1980.

Gorman, Robert. 'Refugee Repatriation in Africa'. *The World Today* 40 (October 1984): 436–433.

Harrell-Bond, Barbara. 'Humanitarianism in a Straitjacket'. *African Affairs* 84, 334 (January 1985): 3–13.

Greenfield, Richard. 'The OAU and Africa's Refugees'. In *The OAU After Twenty Years,* edited by Yassin El-Ayouty. (New York: Praeger, 1984).

Hodges, Tony. 'Africa's Refugee Crisis'. *Africa Report* 29, 1 (January-February 1984): 4–10.

Hamrell, Sven, ed. *Refugee Problems in Africa.* Uppsala, Sweden: SIAS, 1967.

International Council of Voluntary Agencies. *African Refugees: A Challenge to the World.* Geneva, 1981.

Keller, Edmund J., ed. *Issue: A Journal of Africanist Opinion.* Special Issue on African Refugees. 12, 1–2. Spring-Summer, 1982.

Kibreab, Gaim. *Reflections on the African Refugee Problem: A Critical Analysis of Some Basic Assumptions* (Research Report no. 670). Uppsala: SIAS, 1983.

Melander, Goran. *Refugees in Somalia.* Uppsala: SIAS, 1980.

Melander, Goran and Nobel, Peter. *African Refugees and the Law.* Uppsala: SIAS, 1978.

Pitterman, Shelly. 'A Comparative Survey of Two Decades of International Assistance to Refugees in Africa', *Africa Today* 31, 1 (1984):25–54.

UNHCR. *Report on the Conference on the Situation of Refugees in Africa.* REF/AR/CONF/Rpt.I. Arusha, Tanzania: 1979.

World Bank. *Accelerated Development in Sub-Saharan Africa.* Washington, D.C. 1981.

World Bank. *Toward Sustained Development in Sub-Saharan Africa: A Joint Program of Action.* Washington, D.C. 1984.

GENERAL WORKS ON REFUGEES

Brown, Barbara. *Disaster Preparedness and the United Nations Advance Planning for Disaster Relief.* New York: Pergamon Press, 1979.

Chandler, Edgar H.S. *The High Tower of Refuge: The Inspiring Story of Refugee Relief Throughout the World.* New York: Praeger, 1959.

Cuny, Frederick, C. 'The UNHCR and Relief Operations: A Changing role'. *IMR* 15, 1–2 (Spring-Summer 1981): 16–19.

Ferris, Elizabeth. *Refugees in World Politics.* New York: Praeger, 1985.

Gallagher, Dennis, ed., Special Issue of *IMR* entitled 'Refugees: Issues and Directions', 20 (Summer 1986).

Gordenker, Leon. 'Refugees in Developing Countries and Transnational Organization'. *The Annals* 467 (May, 1983): 62–77.

Grahl-Madsen, Atle. *The Status of Refugees in International Law: Refugee Character.* Vol. I. Leiden, The Netherlands: A.W. Sijthoff, 1966.

Grahl-Madsen. *The Status of Refugees in International Law: Asylum, Entry and Sojourn.* Vol. II. Leiden, The Netherlands: A.W. Sijthoff, 1972.

Green, Stephen. *International Disaster Relief: Toward a Responsive System.* New York: McGraw Hill, 1977.

Hansen, Art and Smith, Anthony Oliver, eds. *Involuntary Migration and Resettlement.* Boulder, Co.: Westview 1982.

Holborn, Louise. *The International Refugee Organization. A Specialized Agency of the United Nations: Its History and Work, 1946–1952.* London: Oxford University Press, 1956.

Holborn, Louise. *Refugees, A Problem of Our Time: The Work of the High Commissioner for Refugees, 1952–1972.* 2 vols. Metuchen: The Scarecrow Press, 1975.

Independent Commission on International Humanitarian Issues. *Famine: A Man-made Disaster?* (New York: Vintage Books,1985).

Kritz, Mary. ed., *U.S. Immigration and Refugee Policy*. Lexington, Mass.: D.C. Heath, 1983.

Loescher, Gilburt and Loescher, Ann. *The World's Refugees: A Test of Humanity*. New York: Harcourt Brace Jovanovich. 1982.

Loescher, Gilburt D. and Scanlan, John A., eds. *The Global Refugee Problem: U.S. and World Response*. Special Issue of The Annals. 467 Beverly Hills: Sage, May 1983.

Newland, Kathleen. *Refugees: The New International Politics of Displacement*. Worldwatch Institute Papers. No. 43. Unipub, 1981.

Price, Charles A., ed. *Refugees: The Challenge of the Future*. Canberra: Academy of the Social Sciences in Australia, 1981.

Stein, Barry N. and Tomasi, Silvano M., eds. (Special Double Issue on Refugees) *IMR*. 15, 1–2, (Spring-Summer 1981).

Suhrke, Astri. 'Global Refugee Movements and Strategies of Response'. In *U.S. Immigration and Refugee Policy*, edited by Mary M. Kritz. Lexington, Mass.: D.C. Heath, 1983.

Tomasi, Lydio F. ed. *In Defense of the Alien: Refugees and Territorial Asylum*. Vol. V. New York: Center for Migration Studies, 1983.

UNHCR. *Special Report: Refugee Integration*. Geneva: UNHCR Public Information Section, undated.

Zolberg, Aristide. 'Contemporary Transnational Migrations in Historical Perspective: 'Patterns and Dilemmas'. In Mary Kritz, ed. *U.S. Immigration and Refugee Policy*. Lexington, Mass.: D.C. Heath, 1983.

WORKS ON NGOS IN REFUGEE AID AND DEVELOPMENT

Bolling, Landum and Smith, Craig. *Private Foreign Aid: U.S. Philantropy for Relief and Development*. Boulder, Co: Westview Press,1982.

Brown, Mark Malloch,'The Rise and Rise of the Volag'. *The Development Report* (August, 1984): 1–2.

Ellis, Gene. 'Making PVOs Count More: A Proposal'. In *Private Voluntary Organizations as Agents of Development*, edited by Robert Gorman. Boulder, CO: Westview, 1984.

Forsythe, David. *Humanitarian Politics: The International Committee for the Red Cross*. Baltimore, Md.: Johns Hopkins University Press, 1977.

Gorman, Robert. 'Private Voluntary Organization and Refugee Relief'. In *Refugees in World Politics*, edited by Elizabeth Ferris. New York: Praeger, 1985.

Gorman, Robert. *Private Voluntary Organizations as Agents of Development*. Boulder, Co.: Westview, 1984.

Jones, Mervyn. *In Famine's Shadow: A Private War on Hunger*. Boston: Beacon Press, 1965.

Linden, Eugene. *The Alms Race: The Impact of American Voluntary Aid Abroad*. New York: Random House, 1976.

Lissner, Jorgen. *The Politics of Altruism: A Study of the Political Behavior of Voluntary Development Agencies.* Geneva: Lutheran World Federation, 1977.

OECD. *Directory of Non-governmental Organizations in OECD Member Countries Active in Development Cooperation.* Paris, 1981.

Schwartz, Elliott, *Private Voluntary Organizations in Development in Foreign Aid.* Washington, D.C.: Office of Management and Budget, 1976.

Sommer, John. *Beyond Charity: U.S. Voluntary Aid for A Changing World.* Washington, D.C.: Overseas Development Council, 1977.

Tendler, Judith. *Turning Voluntary Organizations into Development Agencies: Questions for Evaluation.* Evaluation Discussion paper No. 12. Washington, D.C.: AID, 1982.

UNDP. 'Note on Procedures for Contracting with NGOs'. New York, 1985.

DOCUMENTS

Federal Republic of Germany. Statement delivered at ICARA II. Geneva, Switzerland. July 1984.

Finland, Statement delivered at ICARA II. Geneva, Switzerland. July 1984.

United Kingdom. *Terms of Reference: ICARA II Refugee-Related Infrastructure Projects.* London: Overseas Development Administration, 1984.

United Kingdom. Statement delivered at ICARA II. Geneva, Switzerland. July 1984.

UNDP. Annual Reports of the Administrator.

UNGA. Second International Conference on Assistance to Refugees in Africa. *Detailed Description of Needs, Project Outlines, and Background Information on the Refugee Situation.* A/CONF.125/2. 23 March 1984.

UNGA. *Report of the Secretary-General on the Second International Conference on Assistance to Refugees in Africa.* A/39/402/Add.1. 5 November 1984.

United States. Statement delivered at ICARA II. Geneva, Switzerland. July 1984.

U.S. Congress. *Congressional Record* 98th and 99th Congress. Vols 130 and 131.

U.S. Congress. *Legislation on Foreign Relations Through 1978.* Vol. I. February 1979.

U.S. Statement to the Conference on the African Emergency, Geneva, Switzerland. March, 1985.

U.S. Migration and Refugee Act of 1962. PL 87-510, 76 Stat. 121.

U.S. Refugee Act of 1980. PL 96-212. 94 Stat. 109.

World Bank. Statement to ICARA II. July 1984.

World Food Program. Statement to ICARA II. Geneva, Switzerland. July 1984.

OTHER REFERENCES AND SOURCES CONSULTED

Archer, Angus. 'Methods of Multilateral Management: The Interrelationship of International Organizations and NGOs'. In *The United States, the United*

200

Nations, and the Management of Global Change edited by Toby Gati. New York: New York University Press, 1983.

Africa Research Bulletin, 15 May 1981.

European Communities. *The Courier.* 89 (January-February 1985).

Ernst Gohlert. 'The Advisory Committee on Voluntary Foreign Aid and the Non-governmental Liaison Service: A Case Study in Organization and Development'. Paper presented at the International Studies Association Meetings, Washington, D.C. March 1984.

ICVA News (Geneva, Switzerland).

Interfaith Action for Economic Justice Policy. *Notes.*

International Refugee Integration Resource Centre (IRIRC). *International Bibliography of Refugee Literature.* Geneva, 1985.

Pei-heng, Chiang. *Non-Governmental Organizations at the United Nations: Identity, Role, Function.* New York: Praeger, 1983.

UNHCR. *Refugees Magazine.*

U.S. Committee for Refugees, *World Refugee Survey* New York. Published annually, 1964–1984 (annual reports).

U.S. Department of State. *United States Contributions to International Oranizations: Report to the Congress for Fiscal Year 1983.* 32nd Annual Report. Washington, D.C.: 1983.

Wall Street Journal.

Washington Post.

Index

202

Campus	Pol.	~~EAC~~ Donneurs Eng	GR	NGA	Tot
1	(N)		FR	FR	(FR)
2	N		FR		
3	N		FR		
4	N		FR		
			Total		
Pop gén	N				